MAIN CHARACTER MONEY

The Money Talk Nobody Gave You

By Joseph Maxim

Legal Notice

The information contained in this book is based on research and personal experience. The author has made every effort to ensure the accuracy and completeness of the information contained within this book. However, the author does not warrant that the information is free of errors, complete, or current. The author shall not be held liable for any loss, damage, or disruption caused by errors or omissions, whether such errors or omissions result from negligence, accident, or any other cause. Laws, regulations, tax codes, and financial products change frequently. While we have made every effort to present current information as of the publication date, some details may have changed since printing. Readers are encouraged to verify current rules and regulations, particularly regarding tax laws, contribution limits, and financial products, before making financial decisions.

A note on numbers: Tax brackets, standard deductions, retirement account contribution limits (401(k), TSP, IRA, HSA), and income thresholds for Roth IRA eligibility are adjusted by the IRS annually for inflation. The specific numbers in this book reflect 2026 figures. Before making decisions based on these limits, verify the current year's numbers at IRS.gov or consult a tax professional. The *principles* in this book remain constant even as the specific dollar amounts change.

Disclaimer

conditions. The characters in this book are fictional composites inspired by real financial situations. Any resemblance to specific individuals is coincidental.

Affiliate Relationships: This book may mention specific products, services, or companies. The author has no financial relationship with these entities and receives no compensation for mentioning them. Any product or service mentioned is included solely because the author believes it may be helpful to readers.

Introduction: Why This Book Exists

Michael is twenty-six years old, makes $55,000 a year in IT support, and has $87 in his savings account.

That's not a typo. Eighty-seven dollars.

He also has $8,000 in credit card debt across two credit cards, a car payment he probably shouldn't have taken on, and a vague sense that he's supposed to be doing something with a 401(k), whatever that is. He's not dumb. He graduated college, landed a decent job, shows up every day, does good work. But when it comes to money, he's been running on vibes and crossed fingers since the day he got his first real paycheck.

Last Tuesday, a coworker mentioned—casually, over lunch—that she'd just hit $40,000 in her investment portfolio. She's the same age as Michael. Same company. Similar salary.

Michael didn't say anything. He just nodded and changed the subject. But for the rest of the afternoon, he couldn't focus. He kept running the math in his head—he'd been working for four years and had nothing. She'd been working the same amount of time and had forty grand invested. Same job. Same salary. What the hell had he been doing?

The realization that he should know this stuff by now. And he doesn't.

Now let me tell you about Tyler.

Tyler is eighteen. He just graduated high school, lives at home, and works part-time at a warehouse making $14 an hour. He has no debt—but he also has no savings, no credit history, no idea what a W-4 is, and nobody in his life who's ever talked to him about money.

Not because his parents were hiding anything. They just didn't have the knowledge to pass on. His mom lives paycheck to paycheck. His dad has been out of the picture since Tyler was nine. Money in Tyler's world has always been something you run out of before the month ends. The idea that it could be something you *build*—that it could work for you instead of against you—has never occurred to him.

Tyler and Michael are standing at different points on the same road. Tyler is at the starting line with nothing. Michael is a few miles in, but heading in the wrong direction.

This book is for both of them. It's for you too.

The Education You Never Got

Here's an uncomfortable truth: the American education system has largely failed to teach financial literacy. You can graduate high school—even college—knowing calculus and the causes of World War I but having no idea how a credit score works, what a 401(k) or TSP is, or why compound interest is either your best friend or worst enemy depending on which side of it you're on.

Only 23 states require high school students to take a personal finance course. And even in those states, the quality varies wildly. Most young adults enter the "real world" knowing essentially nothing about managing money—and are immediately expected to make decisions about student loans, credit cards, insurance, and retirement accounts.

It's like being handed the keys to a car without ever taking a driving lesson, then being blamed when you crash.

This book exists because that education gap is unacceptable. You deserve to understand how money works. Financial stress affects everything—your health, your relationships, your career options, your ability to take risks and pursue the things you actually care about.

Money isn't everything. But not understanding money can cost you everything.

Wealth Starts Somewhere (Usually at Zero)

There's a myth that wealthy people were born that way. Trust fund babies. Silver spoons. Lucky breaks.

Some were. But most weren't.

Howard Schultz built Starbucks after growing up in Brooklyn public housing. Oprah Winfrey rose from rural Mississippi poverty. Do Won Chang immigrated from Korea with almost nothing and worked as a janitor before building Forever 21.

A necessary caveat: These are extreme success stories, and survivorship bias is real — for every billionaire who started with nothing, millions of equally hardworking people didn't reach that level. The point isn't that hard work guarantees wealth. It's that financial security is more achievable than most people believe. At the same time, the playing field isn't level. The median Black family holds about 15 cents for every dollar of white family wealth. Women still earn roughly 82 cents on the dollar. Wage stagnation, housing discrimination, and healthcare costs create barriers that individual financial decisions can't fully overcome. Both things are true: your financial choices matter enormously, *and* the system isn't fair. This book focuses on what you can control while acknowledging what you can't.

The statistics back this up. Roughly 80% of millionaires are first-generation wealthy—they didn't inherit their money. The most common occupations among millionaires aren't celebrities or tech founders; they're engineers, accountants, teachers, and managers. The tools are learnable. The principles are universal.

The gap isn't between "people who are good with money" and "people who aren't." It's between people who've learned the rules and people who haven't.

You're about to learn the rules.

Meet the Cast

You'll follow five people through this book. Each one represents a different starting point, a different set of challenges, and a different version of you. Their stories are fictional composites drawn from real financial situations—the kind of situations millions of people navigate every day. Whatever your circumstances look like right now, you'll recognize yourself in at least one of them.

Tyler — The Fresh Start Age: 18 | Just graduated high school, starting community college, lives at home

Tyler works part-time at a warehouse making $14/hour, bringing in roughly $16,800 a year. He has no debt—but also no savings, no credit history, and no financial education whatsoever. His parents never talked about money—not out of secrecy, but because they were barely keeping their own heads above water. Tyler's advantage: he's starting from zero, not from negative. His challenge: everything about adult money is brand new, and his friend group thinks investing is "something rich people do."

Tyler represents the reader who's catching this early. He's the proof that starting at eighteen—even with almost nothing—changes everything.

Jordan — The Student Loan Survivor Age: 23 | Marketing coordinator, $48K salary, $34K in student loans

Jordan graduated last year with a communications degree and a mountain of federal student loans. She's in her first "real" job, splitting a two-bedroom apartment with a roommate, and trying to figure out what a W-4 is and whether she should enroll in her company's retirement plan when she can barely make minimums on her loans. She's smart, motivated, and overwhelmed.

Jordan represents the reader who did everything "right"—went to college, got the degree, landed the job—and still feels financially behind.

Mia — The Hustler Age: 21 | Two part-time jobs, no degree, no debt, living with three roommates

Mia skipped college and went straight to work. She bartends four nights a week and does freelance social media management during the day. Her income is variable—some months she clears $3,500, others barely $2,000. She has no student debt (a genuine advantage she doesn't fully appreciate yet) but also no benefits, no employer retirement plan, and no safety net.

Mia represents the gig economy reader—resourceful, independent, and navigating a financial system that wasn't designed for people without a single salaried job.

Michael — The Late Awakener Age: 26 | IT support, $55K salary, $8K in credit card debt, spending everything

Michael makes decent money but has nothing to show for it. No savings, no retirement account, and $8,000 in credit card debt from a combination of lifestyle creep, a breakup that cost him a security deposit, and a general philosophy of "I'll figure it out later." Later has arrived. A coworker's casual mention of her investment portfolio triggered a quiet panic he can't shake.

Michael represents the reader who isn't starting from zero—he's starting from behind, and he knows it.

Emma — The Quiet Optimizer Age: 24 | Federal employee (GS-9), $68K salary, contributes to TSP

Emma works for the federal government and is doing "fine." She contributes 5% to her Thrift Savings Plan to get the full agency match, has a savings account with about $4,000 in it, and no debt. But she doesn't know if she's doing enough, doing it right, or missing something obvious. She's never had a financial conversation with anyone and feels embarrassed to ask. The TSP has incredible advantages she's barely tapping—and she doesn't even know what L Fund she's in.

Emma represents the reader who isn't in crisis but senses there's a whole level of financial literacy she's missing. She also represents every federal employee and service member with TSP access who's leaving free money on the table.

You'll see Tyler, Jordan, Mia, Michael, and Emma in every chapter. You'll watch them make decisions—some smart, some not. You'll see their real numbers, their real mistakes, and their real progress. Because personal finance isn't abstract. It's what happens when a specific person with a specific income faces a specific decision on a specific Tuesday afternoon.

Their stories are how you'll learn. The principles are what you'll keep.

What This Book Will (and Won't) Do

This book will:

- Explain personal finance concepts in plain English, without jargon or condescension
- Give you practical, actionable steps you can implement immediately
- Meet you where you are—whether you're starting with nothing or starting with debt
- Show you what financial concepts actually look like in real people's lives, with real numbers
- Be honest about trade-offs and acknowledge that personal finance is *personal*

This book won't:

- Promise you'll get rich quick (spoiler: you won't, and anyone promising that is lying)

- Shame you for past financial mistakes (everyone makes them)
- Pretend there's one "right" way to manage money (there isn't)
- Ignore the real challenges of building wealth on a modest income
- Bore you to death with dense paragraphs of numbers (we use charts for that)

A Note for International Readers

This book is written primarily for a U.S. audience. The specific tax laws, retirement accounts (401(k), TSP, IRA), credit scoring systems, and regulatory frameworks discussed are American systems. However, the core principles—spend less than you earn, build emergency savings, invest for the long term, avoid high-interest debt—are universal.

If you're outside the U.S., the concepts will still apply, but you'll need to research your country's equivalents for retirement accounts, tax-advantaged savings, and credit systems. Many countries have similar structures with different names and rules.

How to Use This Book

You can read this book cover to cover, or you can skip to the chapters most relevant to your current situation. Each chapter stands on its own while building on themes from earlier sections.

Chapter 1: Your Money Story — Understanding your relationship with money, the psychological baggage we all carry, and why mindset matters before tactics.

Chapter 2: The Basics Nobody Explains — Income vs. wealth, taxes explained simply, compound interest (your superpower), inflation, and why your paycheck isn't what you think it is.

Chapter 3: Budgeting Without the Misery — Finding a budgeting approach that fits your life, from 50/30/20 to zero-based to anti-budget methods.

Chapter 4: Building Your Safety Net — Emergency funds: how much you need, where to keep it, and how to build it even when money is tight.

Chapter 5: Debt — The Good, the Bad, and the Crushing — Understanding different types of debt, payoff strategies, when to prioritize debt vs. investing, and your rights with collectors.

Chapter 6: Credit Scores Decoded — How credit scores work, what affects them, how to build credit from scratch, and protecting yourself from identity theft.

Chapter 7: Investing Isn't Just for Rich People — Compound growth, investment types, retirement accounts (including TSP for federal employees and military), how to actually start investing, and why boring wins.

Chapter 8: Adulting Expenses They Don't Warn You About — Insurance essentials, taxes as an adult, and all the random costs that come with being a grown-up.

Chapter 9: Big Purchases Without Big Regrets — Buying cars, renting apartments, and whether homeownership makes sense—with the real math.

Chapter 10: Protecting Future You — Beneficiaries, identity protection, financial scams targeting young people, and the basic legal documents every adult needs.

Chapter 11: Social Media and Your Financial Health — How platforms profit from your insecurity, the comparison trap, and protecting your financial wellbeing online.

Conclusion: Your Financial Game Plan — Pulling it all together into actionable steps you can start today, plus milestones to aim for.

Bonus Resources — Quick reference guides, recommended tools, sample scripts, annual checklists, glossary, and further reading.

Every chapter ends with a **"When It Goes Sideways"** section—real scenarios where things go wrong, why they go wrong, and exactly what to do about it. Because nobody's financial life goes according to plan. The people who build wealth aren't the ones who avoid mistakes. They're the ones who recover from them.

A Note Before We Begin

You might be reading this right after graduation, trying to figure out what comes next. You might be a few years into your career, realizing you should have started this stuff a long time ago. You might be staring at a student loan balance that makes your chest tight, or a credit card statement you've been avoiding for weeks.

Wherever you are, you're in the right place.

Financial security isn't built overnight. It's built through hundreds of small decisions, made consistently, over time. Some of those decisions will be hard. Some months will be harder than others. You'll mess up sometimes—everyone does.

But every step forward counts. Every dollar saved is a dollar working for you instead of against you. Every bit of knowledge is a tool you can use forever.

The fact that you're reading this means you're already ahead of most people. Seriously. Most people never seek out this information. They just... wing it, and hope for the best.

You're not winging it anymore. Let's get started.

Table of Contents

Chapter 1: Your Money Story

I didn't grow up with money, so I understand the psychology of it. When you ain't got it, you overcompensate when you get it. —Cardi B

Michael was standing in line at Chipotle when he saw it — $340 to DoorDash in the last thirty days.

He wasn't even looking for it. He'd opened his banking app to check whether his paycheck had hit yet—it hadn't—and accidentally tapped his transaction history. DoorDash. DoorDash. DoorDash. Uber Eats. DoorDash. Thirty-seven dollars here, twenty-two there, forty-one on a Saturday night when he was too tired to cook but not tired enough to stop scrolling.

Three hundred and forty dollars. On food he barely remembered eating.

He locked his phone and stared at the menu board. He was about to spend another fourteen dollars. He ordered anyway.

That night, on his couch, he opened his Notes app and typed a question he'd never asked himself: *where does my money actually go?* Not the DoorDash specifically—the whole thing. The spending. The not saving. The $8,000 in credit card debt that had built up so slowly he couldn't point to a single purchase that caused it. He'd been avoiding this for years. Every time money came up in conversation, he changed the subject. Every time his credit card bill hit his inbox, he paid the minimum and closed the tab.

Where did this come from?

The way you think about money was probably decided before you were ten years old.

That's not an exaggeration. By the time you hit double digits, you'd already downloaded a whole belief system about money—

what it means, who deserves it, whether it's something to chase or something to fear. And here's the uncomfortable part: nobody sat you down and taught you any of it.

You learned by watching. By listening. By picking up on what made the adults around you stressed, happy, ashamed, or proud. And now those lessons are running in the background like an app you never meant to install and can't figure out how to delete.

Before we get into budgets and investing and all that practical stuff, we need to deal with this first. Because you can have the perfect budget app and still sabotage yourself if your brain is working against you.

Where Your Money Beliefs Came From

Michael grew up in a household where money came in waves. His dad would land a good contract and suddenly the family was eating out three times a week, buying new clothes, talking about vacations. Then the contract would end, and the mood would shift overnight. Silence at dinner. His mom clipping coupons with a tight jaw. The electricity bill getting paid late—paying it meant admitting the wave was over.

Michael absorbed two lessons from this, both of them invisible at the time: first, that money is unpredictable, so you should enjoy it while it's here. Second, that when money gets tight, you don't talk about it—you just push through and hope the next wave comes.

He's been riding those two lessons his entire adult life. Spending when things feel good. Going silent when they don't.

Tyler's experience was different, but the effect was similar. Money simply wasn't a topic in his house. There just wasn't enough of it to discuss. His mom worked two jobs and still ran out of cash before the end of most months. She didn't teach Tyler about savings accounts or credit scores because she didn't have the bandwidth. Survival was the curriculum.

Tyler didn't learn bad money habits. He learned *no* money habits. When he got his first warehouse paycheck—$541 after taxes on what was supposed to be $672—he had no framework for understanding where the rest went or what to do with what remained. So he did what felt natural: he spent it. Not recklessly. Just... without a plan.

Jordan's household was different again. Her parents were educated, middle-class, careful. They paid their bills on time, drove reasonable cars, never carried credit card debt. But they also never *explained* any of it. Money was handled quietly and competently behind the scenes, like plumbing. Jordan knew the house worked. She had no idea how.

When she graduated college with $34,000 in student loans and a $48,000 salary, she had the general sense that she should be responsible with money. She just had no idea what "responsible" actually meant in practice. So she did what her parents modeled: she handled things quietly, made minimum payments, and avoided looking too closely at the numbers—because in her family, not talking about money meant everything was fine.

It wasn't.

Mia's money story was written in hustle. Her mom raised her and two younger siblings alone, working as a home health aide during the day and cleaning offices at night. Money was always scarce, always urgent, always something you grabbed when you could because you never knew when it would dry up.

Mia internalized the hustle. She's twenty-one and already working two jobs, always picking up extra shifts, always saying yes to freelance gigs. She's fierce about earning. But saving? That feels like a luxury for people who don't have to worry about next month's rent. When she has money, the instinct is to use it—

because in her experience, money sitting still is money at risk of being needed for something else.

Emma doesn't have a dramatic money story. That might actually be her biggest obstacle. Her parents were savers. Not rich—her dad was career Army, her mom was a school administrator—but disciplined. They had a budget. They put money into retirement accounts. They paid cash for things.

But they never explained *why*. The habits were modeled, never taught. So Emma absorbed the behavior—she saves, she's careful, she contributes to her TSP because the orientation packet at her federal job said she should—but she doesn't understand the strategy behind any of it. She's doing the right things for no articulable reason, which means she has no idea whether she's doing *enough* of the right things, or whether she's missing something obvious.

She worries about it more than she'd admit. Not in a dramatic way—just a low hum in the back of her head every time she sees a financial headline or hears a coworker mention investing. The worry doesn't push her to learn. It pushes her to avoid the topic entirely, because asking questions would mean admitting she doesn't know.

Five people. Five different money stories. None of them were explicitly taught. All of them are shaping financial decisions every single day.

What's yours?

The Messages You Didn't Know You Received

Beyond your immediate family, there's a whole constellation of influences that shaped your money beliefs:

Cultural and community messages. Different cultures have vastly different relationships with money. Some emphasize saving and sacrifice. Others emphasize generosity and sharing wealth. Some treat discussing money as taboo. Others are openly transactional. None of these approaches is universally right or wrong, but they all leave fingerprints on how you operate.

Religious or moral frameworks. "Money is the root of all evil" gets misquoted so often it's become cultural wallpaper. (The actual quote, for what it's worth, is about the *love* of money, not money itself. But that nuance tends to get lost.) Whether you grew up with explicit religious teachings about wealth or just absorbed the general cultural vibe that rich people are probably morally suspect, these messages stick.

Class and economic background. Whether you grew up broke, comfortable, or wealthy shapes everything—what feels "normal" to spend, what feels possible to achieve, how scary financial risk feels. Tyler, growing up in a household where money was always tight, has a fundamentally different relationship with a savings account than Emma, who grew up watching her parents quietly build one. Neither is wrong. But both are carrying assumptions they didn't choose.

Social media's funhouse mirror. This one is uniquely powerful for this generation. Comparing your behind-the-scenes to everyone else's highlight reel warps your sense of what's normal and attainable. Michael's coworker who triggered his panic? Michael has no idea whether she inherited money, lives with her parents rent-free, or built that portfolio from scratch on the same salary. He just knows the number, and the number made him feel behind.

We'll dig deeper into social media's specific financial traps in Chapter 11—it deserves its own conversation.

Common Money Mindsets (And Their Traps)

Most people fall into recognizable patterns with money. Our cast illustrates them perfectly—but see if you recognize yourself too:

The Avoider

How it sounds: "I'll check my bank account later. I don't want to know. If I don't look at it, maybe it's fine."

Where it comes from: Often rooted in anxiety or past financial trauma. Looking at the numbers feels threatening, so not looking becomes a form of self-protection.

The trap: Avoidance feels safe in the moment but creates bigger problems over time. Bills go unpaid. Overdrafts stack up. Small issues become emergencies. The thing you were avoiding to protect your peace ends up destroying it.

Who this looks like: Jordan. She pays her student loan minimums on autopay specifically so she never has to look at the balance. Her bank sends her low-balance alerts that she swipes away without reading. She tells herself this is fine because the bills are getting paid. But she's flying blind.

The irony: Avoiders often spend *more* mental energy worrying vaguely about money than they would spend just... looking at it.

The Spender

How it sounds: "Life is short. I deserve this. I'll figure out the money part later. You can't take it with you!"

Where it comes from: Sometimes it's a reaction to deprivation—growing up without, then overcorrecting when you finally have your own money. Sometimes it's emotional regulation—buying things creates a dopamine hit that temporarily numbs stress, boredom, or sadness. Sometimes it's genuine optimism taken too far.

The trap: Future You is a real person who has to deal with the consequences of Present You's decisions. "Later" always arrives. And spending to feel better creates a cycle—the temporary high fades, the guilt kicks in, and you spend again to escape the guilt.

Who this looks like: Michael. His $340 DoorDash month wasn't a one-time thing. It was a pattern. The spending isn't about food—it's about the feeling. Comfort. Ease. A small reward at the end of a day he didn't love. The credit card debt didn't happen from one bad purchase. It happened from a thousand small ones he barely noticed.

The tell: If you've ever hidden an Amazon box or felt your stomach drop looking at your credit card statement, you might be in spender territory.

The Hoarder

How it sounds: "I can't spend money on that. What if I need it for something important? Better to save just in case."

Where it comes from: Usually anxiety-driven, often rooted in past instability or scarcity. Saving provides a sense of control and security in an unpredictable world.

The trap: Money is a tool, and tools are meant to be used. Hoarding to the point where you can't enjoy life, can't make reasonable purchases, can't invest in yourself or your experiences—that's the anxiety running the show, not wisdom. There's a difference between prudent saving and fear-based deprivation.

Who this looks like: Tyler could easily end up here. He grew up watching his mom run out of money every month. Once he starts saving—once he feels the security of that $500 for the first time—the instinct to protect it at all costs will be strong. The concert tickets WIGS in Chapter 4 is his first brush with it: he'd rather lose a friendship than touch his savings. That protectiveness is understandable. It becomes a problem when it stops you from investing, spending on things that genuinely matter, or living your life.

The irony: Some hoarders have way more saved than their friends and still feel broke. The number is never high enough to quiet the fear because the fear isn't really about the number.

The Worrier

How it sounds: "I know I'm probably fine, but I still feel anxious about money constantly. I check my accounts multiple times a day. I run the numbers over and over."

Where it comes from: General anxiety that latches onto money as its focus. Money is an easy target—it's quantifiable, it's important, and there's always something to worry about.

The trap: Worrying and planning are not the same thing. You can spend hours ruminating without taking a single productive action. The worry feels like work, but it's not. It's just suffering.

Who this looks like: Emma, to a degree. She checks her bank balance almost daily. She's not in trouble—she just has this nagging feeling that something's wrong and she can't pin down what. She's not worried about running out of money. She's worried about doing it wrong. The checking is a compulsion, not a strategy.

The distinction: Productive financial thinking means making a plan and executing it. Unproductive financial worry means cycling through the same fears repeatedly without resolution.

The Ostrich

How it sounds: "I have a job. It's fine. I don't need a budget—I'm not broke."

Where it comes from: Sometimes genuine privilege. Sometimes overconfidence. Sometimes just the discomfort of looking at unsexy logistics.

The trap: Income isn't the same as wealth. People with solid incomes go broke all the time because they assume making money means they don't need a plan. Then one car repair or job loss later, they're scrambling—having spent months making decent money with nothing to show for it.

Who this looks like: Michael again—before the Chipotle moment. He made $55,000 a year. That felt like enough. He never sat down with his numbers because he assumed a decent salary meant he was fine. He wasn't.

The wake-up call: Income is what you earn. Wealth is what you keep. They're related but not the same.

Here's the thing: most people aren't purely one type. You might be an avoider with your student loans but a spender with your credit card. A hoarder about savings but an ostrich about retirement planning. These patterns are situational, and they can shift over time.

The point isn't to label yourself. It's to notice your patterns so you can work with them instead of being run by them.

Rewriting Your Story

Okay, so you've got some unhelpful money patterns. Maybe several. Now what?

First, some good news: awareness is actually half the battle here. Most people go their entire lives on autopilot with money, never questioning why they do what they do. Just by reading this chapter and being honest with yourself, you're already ahead.

But awareness without action is just overthinking. Let's talk about how to actually change things.

Step 1: Identify Your Triggers

A trigger is anything that sets off an automatic financial behavior—especially an unhelpful one.

Common triggers include:

- **Stress:** Rough day at work, so you "deserve" takeout and online shopping

- **Social situations:** Friends suggest an expensive outing and you say yes even though you can't afford it
- **Boredom:** Scrolling turns into buying because you need dopamine
- **Celebration:** Good news means time to treat yourself (even if "treating yourself" is your response to bad news too)
- **Late-night scrolling:** 2 AM + your phone + saved payment info = decisions you regret by morning
- **Shame spiral:** You overspent, feel guilty, avoid looking at your accounts, feel more anxious, spend again to feel better, repeat

Michael's primary trigger is boredom and low-level exhaustion. He doesn't binge-spend. He drip-spends—a DoorDash here, an Amazon impulse buy there—every time his energy dips and his brain wants a quick reward. Once he identified the pattern, he started noticing it in real time. Not always fast enough to stop it. But fast enough to see it.

Mia's trigger is scarcity anxiety. When a good freelance check comes in, her instinct is to spend it before it "disappears"—a holdover from growing up in a household where surplus money always got absorbed by the next emergency. She's not irresponsible. She's responding to a survival program that no longer matches her reality.

Pay attention over the next few weeks. When you catch yourself making a money decision you later regret, work backwards. What happened right before? What were you feeling? What need were you trying to meet?

You're not judging yourself here. You're collecting data.

Step 2: Separate Your Worth from Your Net Worth

This is the big one, and it takes ongoing practice.

You are not your bank account balance. You are not your debt. You are not your salary. You are not your credit score.

These numbers describe your current financial situation. They don't describe your value as a human being.

This might seem obvious stated plainly, but we're constantly fed the message that money equals worth. Rich people are portrayed as smarter, more capable, more deserving. Poor people are portrayed as lazy, irresponsible, failures. These messages are so pervasive they're almost invisible.

But it's nonsense. Good people go broke. Terrible people get rich. Financial success depends heavily on factors outside your control—when you were born, where you were born, what family you were born into, what the economy did, whether you got sick or got lucky, countless variables that have nothing to do with your character.

Michael felt shame when his coworker mentioned her $40,000 portfolio. So what did he do with that shame? He changed the subject and spent the next three weeks pretending the conversation never happened. He didn't open a brokerage account. He didn't google "how to start investing." He ordered DoorDash and watched YouTube until the feeling faded. Shame doesn't motivate people to fix their finances. It motivates them to look away.

Tyler has a net worth of approximately zero. That number says nothing about his work ethic, his potential, or his character. It says he's eighteen and just getting started—which is exactly where most eighteen-year-olds are, whether they know it or not.

When you tie your self-worth to your financial situation, two bad things happen: you feel shame about financial struggles, which makes you avoid dealing with them, which makes them worse. And you make money decisions to protect your ego instead of to serve your actual goals.

You can be a work in progress financially *and* a complete, worthy human being. Both are true at once.

Step 3: Build a Healthier Relationship

What would a healthy relationship with money actually look like?

Money as a tool, not a scorecard. Money is useful. It buys options, security, experiences, comfort. It's a means to ends you care about. It's not a measure of your character.

Engaged but not obsessed. You know what's going on with your finances. You check in regularly. But you don't ruminate constantly or let anxiety run the show. Emma checks her balance every day and it doesn't make her feel better—it's just a nervous habit. Jordan hasn't looked at her student loan balance in six months and tells herself that's fine. Neither approach is working. The goal is somewhere in the middle: informed, not anxious.

Aligned with your values. Your spending reflects what actually matters to you—not what you think should matter, not what marketing told you matters, not what impresses other people. Mia's spending should reflect her independence. Michael cares about experiences. Tyler needs stability before anything else. What you value will shape what "good with money" looks like for you—and it won't look the same as it does for anyone else.

Flexible but boundaried. You can adapt when circumstances change without throwing out all your plans. But you also have non-negotiables that keep you from going completely off track.

Forward-looking but present. You're building for the future without sacrificing all joy in the present. Retirement matters, but so does the life you're living right now.

This isn't a destination you arrive at. It's a practice. You'll have good months and bad months. You'll slip into old patterns sometimes. That's fine. The goal is general trajectory, not perfection.

A Quick Exercise Before We Move On

Open your Notes app or grab whatever's nearby. Answer these honestly—nobody's going to see this but you.

1. Write down three messages about money you absorbed growing up.

These might be explicit things people said ("Money doesn't grow on trees," "We can't afford that," "Rich people are greedy") or implicit lessons you learned from watching ("Money causes fights," "Asking for money is shameful," "Looking successful matters more than being financially stable").

2. For each message, ask: Is this actually true?

Some might be. "Money is finite" is true. "You should spend less than you earn" is generally solid advice. But some might not hold up to examination. "Asking for money is shameful" isn't a universal truth—it's a story. "Rich people are greedy" is a stereotype, not a fact.

3. For each message, ask: Is this serving me?

Even if a belief has some truth to it, it might not be useful. "You should always save as much as possible" might sound wise, but if it's preventing you from investing in your education or enjoying your life, it's not serving you anymore.

4. What would you rather believe instead?

You can't just delete old beliefs—you need to replace them with something better. What money beliefs would actually help you build the life you want?

This exercise isn't magic. You won't finish it and suddenly be reprogrammed. But you'll start noticing things—moments where an old belief is driving a decision you wouldn't consciously choose. That noticing is the first crack in the autopilot.

Your Move

- **Today:** Write down three money messages you absorbed growing up. Just three. Notes app is fine.
- **This week:** Identify which money mindset pattern fits you best. No judgment—just awareness.
- **This month:** Have one honest conversation about money with someone you trust. Doesn't have to be deep. Just honest.

When It Goes Sideways

Real scenarios. Real solutions. No judgment.

"I tried to journal about money and it just made me angry."

What happened: You sat down to examine your money beliefs like the exercise above suggested, and instead of clarity, you felt rage. At your parents for not teaching you. At the system for not preparing you. At yourself for being twenty-something and not knowing this stuff.

Why it happens: Money is emotional. It's tied to safety, identity, family dynamics, and survival. Asking someone to examine their money beliefs is like asking them to examine their childhood—it can surface things you weren't ready for. Anger is often the first layer. Underneath it is usually fear, grief, or shame.

What to do: Let yourself be angry. Don't force it into gratitude or positivity. But also don't let the anger become a reason to stop. Feel it, acknowledge it, and then come back to the work tomorrow. If the emotions are overwhelming—if you're realizing that your relationship with money is tangled up with trauma—that's real, and a financial therapist (yes, that's a thing) can help you sort through it in ways a book can't.

What not to do: Use the anger as evidence that financial self-improvement is pointless. "This is too painful, so I'll just keep winging it" is the avoider pattern wearing a different mask.

"My family's money story is trauma, not just 'beliefs.'"

What happened: The phrases "money beliefs" and "money mindset" feel inadequate for what you actually experienced. You didn't just absorb messages about money. You lived through poverty, instability, eviction, food insecurity, or worse. Your money story isn't a story—it's a survival record.

Why it happens: Because for some people, financial stress wasn't background noise—it was the dominant experience of childhood. And the coping mechanisms you developed to survive that environment are deeply wired. They don't dissolve because someone tells you to "think differently about money."

What to do: Go slowly. You don't need to unpack everything at once. Start with one small, concrete action—opening a savings account, setting up a $10 automatic transfer, reading the next chapter—that proves to your nervous system that engaging with money can be safe. If the emotional weight is heavy, a therapist who understands financial trauma (look for financial therapy or financial counseling credentials) can help you separate the survival responses from the present-day reality.

What not to do: Compare your starting point to anyone else's. Tyler and Mia both carry financial trauma. Their paths forward will look different from Emma's or Jordan's. That's not a disadvantage—it's just a different starting line. The destination is the same.

"I know my money mindset is broken but I can't change it."

What happened: You've identified your patterns. You see the avoidance, the spending, the anxiety. You understand intellectually where it comes from. But nothing changes. You keep doing the same things.

Why it happens: Because awareness and behavior change are two different skills. Knowing why you overspend doesn't automatically stop you from overspending, just like knowing cigarettes are unhealthy doesn't automatically make someone quit. The neural pathways are grooved deep.

What to do: Stop trying to change the mindset first. Change the *system* first. The rest of this book is about building systems—automated savings, budget frameworks, debt payoff plans—that work even when your brain is being a mess. Michael doesn't need to cure his emotional spending before he can start saving. He needs an automated transfer that moves $100 to a savings account on payday, before he ever sees it. The behavior creates the new mindset over time. Not the other way around.

What not to do: Wait until you feel "ready" or until your relationship with money is "healthy" before taking action. You'll be waiting forever. Start with the systems. Let the feelings catch up.

Alright. You know where your money mindset came from. You've spotted some of your patterns. You've started questioning whether your inherited beliefs are actually serving you. **Now let's get practical.**

Chapter 2: The Basics Nobody Explains

> *"I didn't learn about money in school. I learned about money when I didn't have it." —Daymond John*

Tyler opened his first real paycheck on his phone in the warehouse parking lot.

He'd been working for two weeks—forty hours each—at $14 an hour. He'd done the math in his head before his first shift: two weeks, eighty hours, $1,120. He was going to open a savings account, maybe buy some new work boots, take his mom to dinner.

His direct deposit was $897.

He stared at the number, backed out, and opened the app again. Same number. He scrolled down to the breakdown and saw lines he didn't recognize: Federal Withholding, Social Security, Medicare, State Tax. Each one had taken a bite. Together, they'd eaten $223 of his money before he ever saw it.

Tyler didn't know what half those lines meant. He'd signed something called a W-4 on his first day—his supervisor handed it to him between a stack of safety forms and said "just fill these out"—and he'd checked boxes at random because he didn't want to look stupid by asking questions.

He sat in his car for ten minutes, doing nothing. Then he drove home and didn't mention the paycheck to anyone.

Somewhere between "I got the job!" and "wait, where did my money go?" there's a gap. A big one. It's filled with stuff that everyone assumes you already know—taxes, deductions, how bank accounts actually work, why your balance lies to you. Nobody sits you down and explains any of it. You're just supposed to figure it out while also, you know, surviving.

This chapter is the explanation you never got. It's not complicated, but it matters. Because you can't manage money you don't understand.

Your Paycheck: Where It Actually Goes

Tyler's confusion in that parking lot is universal. Almost everyone is shocked the first time they see the gap between what they earn and what they take home. Let's walk through it using real numbers from our cast.

Your salary or hourly rate is your *gross* income—the number before anyone takes their cut. Your *net* income (also called take-home pay) is what actually lands in your bank account. Those are two very different numbers, and the difference between them is where most people's financial confusion begins.

Here's what happens to your paycheck before you ever see it:

Federal Income Tax

The federal government takes a percentage based on how much you earn. The U.S. uses a progressive tax system, which means higher portions of your income get taxed at higher rates. But here's what most people get wrong: if you move into a higher tax bracket, only the money *above* that threshold gets taxed at the higher rate. Your whole paycheck doesn't suddenly get taxed more.

Jordan almost turned down a raise because of this myth. Her coworker told her a raise would "put her in a higher bracket" and she'd actually take home less. That coworker was wrong—and this misunderstanding might be the most expensive myth in personal finance.

Here's how tax brackets actually work:

2026 Federal Income Tax Brackets (Single Filer)

Taxable Income	Tax Rate
$0 – $12,400	10%
$12,401 – $50,400	12%
$50,401 – $105,700	22%
$105,701 – $201,775	24%
$201,776 – $256,225	32%
$256,226 – $640,600	35%
$640,601+	37%

These brackets apply *after* the standard deduction ($16,100 for single filers in 2026) reduces your taxable income.

Now let's see what this looks like for Jordan and Michael:

Jordan's Tax Calculation ($48,000 salary)

Bracket	Taxable Amount	Rate	Tax
First $12,400	$12,400	10%	$1,240
$12,401 – $31,900	$19,500	12%	$2,340
Total Federal Tax			**$3,580**
Effective Tax Rate			**11.2%**

Jordan's taxable income after the standard deduction: $48,000 – $16,100 = $31,900.

Her *marginal* rate is 12%. That's the rate on her last dollar earned. Her *effective* rate—what she actually pays as a percentage of her full income—is 7.5%. Big difference.

What If Jordan Gets a $7,000 Raise?

Her new salary: $55,000. Taxable income: $38,900. She's crossed into... still the 12% bracket. Her tax goes up by $840, but her income went up by $7,000. She takes home an extra $6,160.

Even if the raise pushed her into the 22% bracket, only the dollars *above* $50,400 in taxable income would be taxed at 22%. The rest stays at the lower rates. You will never, ever take home less money because a raise "put you in a higher bracket." Always take the raise.

State Income Tax

Depends entirely on where you live. Some states take a significant cut—California's top rate is 13.3%, and New York's is 10.9% (plus New York City tacks on an extra 3.9%). Others like Texas, Florida, and Nevada have no state income tax at all. This is a legit factor when deciding where to live—a $50,000 salary goes further in Austin than in San Francisco, and taxes are part of that equation.

Social Security Tax (6.2%)

This funds retirement benefits for current retirees—and eventually for you. Will Social Security exist when you retire? Almost certainly yes, though the exact benefits may be adjusted. The program has broad political support, and Congress has historically stepped in to shore it up when needed. The most likely scenario is that benefits might be slightly reduced or the retirement age might increase—not that the program disappears entirely. Don't count on Social Security as your *only* retirement income, but don't assume it won't be there at all.

Your employer also pays 6.2%, so 12.4% total goes into the system on your behalf.

Unless you're Mia. More on that in a minute.

Medicare Tax (1.45%)

Funds healthcare for people 65 and older. You pay 1.45%, your employer matches it.

Other Possible Deductions

Your paycheck might also show deductions for health insurance premiums (pre-tax, which is actually a good thing), retirement contributions (401(k), TSP, or similar), HSA/FSA contributions, union dues, or wage garnishments.

Emma's pay stub, for example, shows a TSP contribution line—5% of her gross pay goes straight into her Thrift Savings Plan before she ever sees it. What she doesn't know yet: she's contributing to the *traditional* side of her TSP, which reduces her taxable income now but means she'll pay taxes on every dollar she withdraws in retirement. At twenty-four and $68K, she's almost certainly in a lower tax bracket today than she will be at fifty. The smarter move for someone her age? The *Roth* TSP—contributions are taxed now (at her current lower rate), but every dollar of growth comes out tax-free in retirement. One catch: the 5% agency match still goes into traditional TSP no matter what. She can't control that part. But she can flip her own contributions to Roth with one form. We'll break this down fully in Chapter 7.

What This Actually Looks Like: Tyler's Paycheck vs. Reality

Tyler expected $1,120 for his two-week pay period. Here's what actually happened:

Tyler's Biweekly Paycheck Breakdown ($14/hr, 80 hours)

Line Item	Amount
Gross Pay	$1,120.00
Federal Income Tax	−$78.00
Social Security (6.2%)	−$69.44
Medicare (1.45%)	−$16.24
State Income Tax	−$39.00

Line Item	Amount
Net Pay (Take-Home)	**$917.32**

Tyler doesn't have health insurance through work (he's still on his mom's plan until he turns 26) and hasn't enrolled in any retirement plan, so his deductions are relatively simple. But that $203 gap between what he earned and what he got? That's the tax system at work. It's not theft. It funds roads, schools, Social Security, Medicare, the military. But if you don't know it's coming, it feels like someone took your money.

Now compare Tyler's situation to the rest of the cast:

Paycheck Reality Check: Monthly Take-Home

Estimates based on 2026 tax rates; actual take-home varies by state, deductions, and filing status.

Character	Gross Annual	Gross Monthly	Estimated Monthly Take-Home	Lost to Taxes & Deductions
Tyler	$16,800	$1,400	$1,190	$210 (15%)
Jordan	$48,000	$4,000	$3,200	$800 (20%)
Mia	$30,000 (variable)	$2,500	$2,500*	$0 upfront*
Michael	$55,000	$4,583	$3,550	$1,033 (23%)
Emma	$68,000	$5,667	$3,850**	$1,817 (32%)**

**Mia receives her full amount—no taxes are withheld. She's responsible for setting aside and paying her own.*

***Emma's take-home is lower because she contributes 5% to TSP and pays FERS (Federal Employees Retirement System) retirement contributions on top of standard taxes.*

That asterisk next to Mia's name is important. Let's talk about it.

The Self-Employment Tax Trap: Mia's Problem

When Jordan or Michael get paid, their employer handles half of Social Security and Medicare taxes. The employer pays 7.65%, the employee pays 7.65%, and everyone moves on.

Mia doesn't have an employer. She *is* the employer. That means she pays both halves: the full 15.3% self-employment tax on top of her regular income tax. Her bartending gig withholds taxes like a regular job, but her freelance social media work? Every dollar arrives in her bank account untouched. No deductions. No withholding. Just the full amount sitting there looking like more money than it actually is.

Here's what Mia owes on $15,000 in freelance income:

Mia's Freelance Tax Obligation

Tax Type	Rate	Amount
Self-Employment Tax (Social Security + Medicare)	15.3%	$2,295
Federal Income Tax (estimated)	10%	$1,500
State Income Tax (estimated)	4%	$600
Total Tax Owed		**$4,395**
Percentage of Freelance Income		**29%**

Almost thirty cents of every freelance dollar Mia earns belongs to the government. If she doesn't set it aside as she earns it, she'll owe thousands at tax time—money she's already spent.

The IRS expects self-employed people to pay quarterly estimated taxes (April 15, June 15, September 15, January 15). Miss those payments and you'll owe penalties on top of the tax itself.

Mia didn't know any of this for her first year of freelancing. We'll revisit what happened in "When It Goes Sideways."

The W-4: That Form You Rushed Through

Tyler isn't the only one who filled out his W-4 blindly. Most people do. But that form determines how much federal tax gets pulled from each paycheck. Fill it out wrong, and you'll either:

Have too little withheld: Paychecks feel bigger all year. Then tax season arrives and you owe the IRS hundreds or thousands you already spent.

Have too much withheld: Paychecks are smaller than necessary, but you get a big refund in April.

That refund might feel like a gift, but it's not. It's your own money that you gave the government an interest-free loan of for twelve months. A $2,400 refund means you overpaid by $200 every month—money that could have been paying down debt or sitting in a savings account earning interest.

The goal isn't the biggest possible refund. The goal is to break even—owe nothing, get nothing (or close to it). The IRS has a free withholding estimator online that takes about fifteen minutes and tells you exactly how to fill out your W-4 to hit that target.

When to update your W-4: when you start a new job, get married or divorced, have a kid, start a side hustle with significant income, buy a house, or if last year you owed a lot or got a huge refund.

Your Bank Account Lies to You

You check your balance. It says $847. Cool, you can afford that $60 dinner with friends tonight.

Except... can you?

Your *available balance* is what the bank says you can spend right now. Your *actual balance* is what's really in your account after all transactions clear. The problem: these numbers are often different.

Pending transactions—charges authorized but not fully processed—might show up in your available balance. They might not. That gas station charge from this morning? The subscription that bills tomorrow? Your rent check that hasn't cleared? All of them are messing with your number.

Michael learned this the expensive way. He checked his balance on a Friday night, saw $340, and spent freely over the weekend—dinner, drinks, an impulse buy at Target. Monday morning, three pending charges from Thursday cleared and his account went negative. Two overdraft fees at $35 each. A $12 sandwich just cost him $82.

The Overdraft Trap

Banks make billions from overdraft fees. You swipe your card for something that pushes you below $0. Instead of declining the transaction, the bank covers it—and charges you $35 for the favor. Buy a $4 coffee when you're $2 short? That's now a $39 coffee.

Some banks charge for *every* transaction that goes through while you're negative. Five small purchases in a day? That's potentially $175 in fees.

The good news: the landscape is shifting. Capital One, Ally Bank, Chime, and Discover have eliminated overdraft fees entirely. Many credit unions have lower or no fees. If you're at a bank still charging $35 per overdraft, switching could save you hundreds a year.

How to protect yourself:

Turn off overdraft "protection" (yes, it's annoying to have your card declined, but less annoying than a $35 fee). Set up low-balance alerts so your phone buzzes when you drop below $100. Keep a mental buffer—pick a number like $200 and treat it as your personal zero. If your balance hits $200, you're "out of money" even though technically you're not.

Fixed vs. Variable Expenses (And the Sneaky Third Kind)

Some expenses are predictable. Others aren't. And a third kind—the one that wrecks most budgets—is predictable but irregular.

Fixed expenses cost the same every month: rent, car payment, insurance premiums, subscriptions, phone bill, student loan payment, internet. Easy to plan for. Jordan's rent is $875 on the first of every month. No surprises.

Variable expenses change based on your behavior: groceries, gas, dining out, entertainment, shopping. This is where budgets usually fall apart. Tyler tells himself he'll spend $200 on food this month. By the twenty-third, he's at $290 and not sure how.

Irregular but predictable expenses are the budget killers nobody warns you about. They don't hit every month, but they're coming:

The Expenses Nobody Budgets For

Expense	Frequency	Estimated Cost
Car registration/inspection	Annual	$100–$400
Holiday gifts	Annual	$200–$800
Dental cleanings	Twice yearly	$100–$200 each
Car maintenance (oil, tires, brakes)	Varies	$500–$1,500/year
Annual subscriptions (software, apps)	Annual	$50–$300
Clothing/shoes	Seasonal	$300–$800/year
Haircuts	Monthly to quarterly	$20–$100 each
Medical copays	Sporadic	$25–$75 per visit
Estimated Annual Total		**$1,300–$4,000+**

The fix: Add up your annual irregular expenses, divide by twelve, and set that amount aside each month in a sinking fund. If your irregular expenses total roughly $2,400 a year, that's $200/month. When the car registration hits, the money's already there. No panic, no credit card, no scrambling.

Emma set up sinking funds after her first year of adulting, when her car registration ($380), a dental bill ($175), and holiday gifts ($400) all hit within six weeks and wiped out most of her savings. She now has separate savings buckets for each category. It took her twenty minutes to set up and it's prevented three minor financial crises since.

Needs vs. Wants (It's More Complicated Than You Think)

Every budgeting guide tells you to separate needs from wants. The basic idea is useful. Rent is a need. A new gaming console is a want. But real life is messier than that.

Internet: Need or want? If you need it for work, job applications, healthcare portals, or online classes—it's a need. Your great-aunt might say "we didn't have internet in my day." Irrelevant. The world runs on it now.

A car: Depends entirely on where you live. In NYC with robust public transit? Probably a want. In suburban Texas where the nearest grocery store is fifteen miles away? It's a need. Tyler needs a car to get to the warehouse. Jordan takes the bus.

Mental health spending: Therapy, a gym membership, the occasional social outing. These might look like wants on a spreadsheet, but if they keep you functional, they're closer to needs.

Instead of rigidly categorizing every expense, ask yourself three questions: Does this serve a real purpose in my life? Am I spending the right *amount* on this purpose? (You need a phone. You don't need the most expensive phone every year.) Am I spending on this intentionally, or out of habit, impulse, or social pressure?

The goal isn't to eliminate all wants. The goal is to spend on the wants that actually matter to you, cut the ones that don't, and make sure your needs are covered first.

The Latte Factor (And Why It's Not the Whole Story)

You've probably heard some version of this: "If you just stopped buying coffee every day, you'd be rich!"

The math usually goes: $5/day × 365 = $1,825/year. Invest that for 30 years and you'd have $200,000!

Technically true. But shaming yourself for small pleasures isn't a sustainable financial strategy. If that daily coffee brings you joy, helps you function, and fits within your budget—keep the coffee.

The *real* insight behind the latte factor isn't "never buy coffee." It's this: **small, thoughtless, habitual spending adds up—especially when it's not actually bringing you joy.**

The problem isn't the $5 coffee you love. It's the $5 coffee you grab out of habit even though it's mediocre. It's the three streaming services you're paying for but only use one. It's the subscription boxes you forgot you signed up for.

Michael discovered he was paying for a gym membership ($49/month), an app he hadn't opened in four months ($9.99/month), and a streaming service he forgot he had ($15.99/month). That's $900 a year on things he wasn't using. Not cutting back on things he loved—eliminating things he'd literally forgotten about.

The Flip Side: Big Expenses Matter More

While you're stressing about lattes, don't ignore the elephant in the room: your biggest expenses have the biggest impact. Housing, transportation, and food typically eat 50–70% of most people's budgets. Getting a roommate saves $500–$1,000/month. Getting a reliable used car instead of a new one saves tens of thousands over time.

Where the Money Actually Goes: Young Adult Budget (Median)

Category	% of Take-Home	Tyler ($1,190/mo)	Jordan ($3,200/mo)	Michael ($3,550/mo)
Housing	30–35%	$350 (at home)*	$875	$1,200
Transportation	10–15%	$200	$150	$485 (car payment) + $180
Food	10–15%	$250	$400	$550
Insurance	5–10%	$0**	$180	$210
Debt Payments	0–20%	$0	$380 (student loans)	$240 (CC minimums)
Everything Else	15–25%	$190	$415	$285
Savings	5–20%	$200	$0***	$0***

**Tyler lives at home and contributes $350/month to household expenses.*

***Tyler is on his mom's health insurance until 26; car insurance is $200/month included in transportation.*

****Jordan and Michael currently save nothing. That's about to change.*

Focus your energy where the money actually is. Optimizing your coffee habit while ignoring that you're spending 40% of your income on a car you can't afford is like rearranging deck chairs on the Titanic.

Compound Interest: The Force That Changes Everything

This is the single most important concept in this entire book. If you remember nothing else from this chapter, remember this.

Compound interest means you earn interest on your interest. The money you save earns returns, and those returns earn their own returns, and those returns earn returns on the returns. Over time, this snowball effect is staggering.

Tyler is eighteen. If he starts putting $100 a month into an investment account earning an average 8% annual return, here's what happens:

Tyler's $100/Month: The Power of Starting at 18

Age	Years Invested	Total Contributed	Account Value
18	0	$0	$0
25	7	$8,400	$11,200
30	12	$14,400	$23,800
40	22	$26,400	$73,600
50	32	$38,400	$182,900
60	42	$50,400	$427,400
65	47	$56,400	$640,800

Tyler contributes $56,400 of his own money. Compound interest adds *$584,400*. That's not a typo. The interest earned is more than ten times what he put in.

But here's the part that matters most: **when you start changes everything.**

Starting at 18 vs. 23 vs. 28: Same $100/Month, Wildly Different Results

Start Age	Total Contributed by 65	Account Value at 65	Difference from Starting at 18

Start Age	Total Contributed by 65	Account Value at 65	Difference from Starting at 18
18 (Tyler)	$56,400	$640,800	—
23 (Jordan)	$50,400	$427,400	–$213,400
28	$44,400	$282,600	–$358,200

Jordan starts five years after Tyler. She contributes only $6,000 less over her lifetime. But she ends up with $213,400 less. Those five years of compound growth that Tyler got and Jordan didn't? They're worth more than Jordan will contribute in total.

This isn't meant to make Jordan feel bad. It's meant to make Tyler act now. And it's meant to show everyone else: every year you wait costs you more than you think. Start today, even if the amount is small. The amount matters less than the time.

The flip side of compound interest is compound *debt*—and it works exactly the same way, but against you. Michael's $8,000 in credit card debt at 24.99% APR is compounding in the wrong direction. We'll cover that in Chapter 5.

Alright. Now you know where your paycheck goes, why your bank balance lies, and how to think about expenses without losing your mind. You know that Mia needs to set aside 25–30% of her freelance income for taxes. You know that Tyler's $100/month at eighteen is worth more than Jordan's $100/month at twenty-three. And you know that Michael's invisible $900 in forgotten subscriptions was costing him more than his coffee habit.

Your Biggest Financial Asset Isn't in a Bank Account

Everything in this chapter so far has been about understanding the money you already have. But there's a number that matters more than your savings rate, your tax bracket, or your investment returns: what you earn.

Tyler makes $14 an hour. If he gets a $2 raise — the kind that comes from showing up consistently, learning new skills, or moving to a slightly better position — that's $4,160 more per year. On his current income, that raise is a 25% increase. No budget trick, no savings hack, no coupon strategy will ever match that.

Jordan started at $48,000 in marketing. Eighteen months later, she's at $52,000 — a $4,000 raise she got by taking on a project nobody else wanted and delivering results her manager couldn't ignore. She didn't ask for the raise by walking into her boss's office and saying "I deserve more." She asked by saying "I led the Q3 campaign that brought in 40 new accounts. I'd like to discuss adjusting my compensation to reflect that."

The difference matters. "I deserve more" is about feelings. "Here's what I've done" is about evidence. Managers can dismiss feelings. Evidence makes them uncomfortable in a useful way.

The math young people don't run:

Raise Per Hour	Extra Per Year	Extra Over 5 Years	Invested at 7% Over 5 Years
$1/hr	$2,080	$10,400	~$12,100
$2/hr	$4,160	$20,800	~$24,200
$3/hr	$6,240	$31,200	~$36,300

A $2/hour raise, sustained over five years, is $20,800. Invested, it's closer to $24,000. That's a down payment. That's a year of student loan payments. That's an emergency fund and then some. A $3/hour raise — the kind Tyler gets by earning his forklift certification — is over $36,000 in five years.

And here's what nobody tells you at 22: **switching jobs is usually the fastest raise.** The average raise for staying at the same company is 3–4%. The average salary increase for switching jobs is 10–20%. Jordan's $4,000 raise was good. If she'd job-hopped to a similar role at a competitor, she might have landed at $58,000 — a $10,000 jump.

This isn't about being disloyal. It's about understanding that companies budget for retention differently than they budget for recruitment. The money they'll offer to get you in the door is almost always more than the money they'll give to keep you.

Tyler's version of this is simpler but just as real. The warehouse pays $14. The distribution center across town pays $16.50 for the same work. Forklift certification — a weekend course, usually $200–$400 — qualifies him for positions starting at $18–20. His earning potential isn't fixed at $14/hour. It's fixed at $14/hour *at this job, with his current skills*. Both of those are changeable.

Mia's earning path looks different because she's self-employed. Her raises come from charging more per project, dropping low-paying clients, and building skills that command higher rates. When she started freelancing, she charged $25/hour for social media management. After building a portfolio and getting testimonials, she raised her rate to $40. Same hours, 60% more money. The clients who balked were replaced by clients who didn't.

We'll go deeper on career strategy and advanced income-building in the Intelligent Wealth series. But the foundation starts here: your income is the raw material everything else in this book is built on. Protecting it matters. Growing it matters more.

The best budget in the world can only stretch a dollar so far. At some point, you need more dollars.

Your Move

- **Today:** Pull up your most recent pay stub. Find your gross pay, net pay, and every deduction. Know the gap.
- **This week:** If you filled out your W-4 by guessing, go to the IRS Withholding Estimator and fix it. Fifteen minutes.
- **This month:** Run your own compound interest calculation at investor.gov. Put in your age, $100/month, and 7%. Look at the number at 65. That's your motivation.

When It Goes Sideways

"I owe taxes and I don't have the money."

What happened: Mia didn't know she needed to pay quarterly estimated taxes on her freelance income. She spent everything she earned. In April, she filed her taxes and discovered she owed $3,800. She had $340 in her checking account.

Why it happens: Nobody tells freelancers and gig workers about self-employment tax. When you get a regular paycheck, taxes are invisible—your employer handles them. When you're self-employed, those taxes are still owed. They're just not taken out automatically, so the money sits in your account looking like it's yours. It's not. Roughly 25–30% of every freelance dollar belongs to the government.

What to do: Don't ignore the bill—that makes it worse. File your return even if you can't pay in full. The IRS offers payment plans (search "IRS Online Payment Agreement") that let you pay in monthly installments. The interest rate is lower than a credit card. Set up the plan, then immediately fix the system: open a separate savings account labeled "Taxes" and transfer 30% of every freelance payment into it the day you get paid. Set up quarterly estimated payments so this never happens again.

What not to do: Put the tax bill on a credit card at 24.99% APR. The IRS payment plan rate is around 7–8%. Don't ignore notices from the IRS—the penalties compound. And don't stop freelancing because of the tax burden—just build the tax set-aside into your system from now on.

"I filled out my W-4 wrong and got a huge tax bill."

What happened: Tyler claimed too many allowances on his W-4 (he checked boxes at random, remember). His employer withheld almost nothing for federal taxes. He felt rich all year. Then he filed his taxes and owed $1,400.

Why it happens: The W-4 is confusing, especially for someone filling it out for the first time. Most people either guess or copy what their parents told them to do (often outdated advice from the pre-2020 form). The result is either too much withheld (big refund, small paychecks) or too little (bigger paychecks, tax bill in April).

What to do: First, handle the immediate problem. If you owe and can't pay in full, the IRS payment plan is your friend—don't let this go to collections. Then fix the root cause: go to the IRS Tax Withholding Estimator (irs.gov, search "withholding estimator"), spend fifteen minutes with your most recent pay stub, and it'll tell you exactly what to put on a new W-4. Submit the updated form to your employer. You can do this anytime—you don't have to wait until tax season.

What not to do: Panic and over-correct by having way too much withheld. The goal is accuracy, not a giant refund. A $3,000 refund means you overpaid by $250 every month—money that could have been in your pocket.

"Inflation math is depressing—why even bother saving?"

What happened: Emma read an article about inflation averaging 3% per year and ran the numbers. If she puts $500 a month into a savings account earning 4.5%, inflation eats most of the gain. In twenty years, her dollars will buy roughly half of what they buy today. She texted a friend: "What's the point of saving if it all gets eaten by inflation?"

Why it happens: Inflation is real, and the math can be discouraging when you look at savings accounts alone. A dollar saved today *will* buy less in twenty years. That's a fact. It's also an incomplete picture.

What to do: Understand the difference between *saving* and *investing*. Savings accounts protect your money from loss—they're for your emergency fund and short-term goals. They're not meant to beat inflation over decades. That's what investing is for. The stock market has historically returned 8–10% annually before inflation, and roughly 5–7% *after* inflation. Emma's $500/month in a savings account barely treads water. That same $500/month invested in a broad market index fund averages growth that significantly outpaces inflation over time. The compound interest chart earlier in this chapter? Those numbers already assume normal inflation. The growth is real.

What not to do: Use inflation as a reason to spend everything now. "Money is losing value anyway, so I might as well enjoy it" is a common rationalization—and it's the fastest way to end up at forty with nothing. Inflation makes saving harder. It makes *not* saving catastrophic.

Your paycheck is smaller than you expected. Taxes take a bigger bite than you realized. Benefits cost more than you thought. None of that changes by ignoring it—it just means the gap between what you earn and what hits your account stays a mystery.

Now you know what the numbers actually are. That's not depressing—it's the starting point. Every strategy in the rest of this book depends on knowing what you're actually working with.

Next step: making those dollars do what you want.

Chapter 3: Budgeting Without the Misery

> *"A budget isn't about restricting yourself — it's about making room for the things that actually matter to you." — Tiffany Aliche, The Budgetnista*

Michael pulled up his banking app on a Sunday night because he was bored, which was a mistake. He scrolled through October's transactions with the slow dread of someone opening a credit card statement they've been avoiding.

DoorDash: $37. Amazon: $24. DoorDash: $19. Spotify: $11.99. Bar tab: $68. DoorDash: $22. Target: $47. Amazon: $31. Another bar tab: $54. DoorDash: $41.

He kept scrolling. The transactions blurred together. Small charges, all of them. Nothing dramatic. No single purchase he could point to and say *that's where it went wrong*. Just a steady leak, twenty and thirty dollars at a time, adding up to a number he didn't want to calculate.

He calculated it anyway. Non-essential spending for October: $1,340. On a take-home of about $3,550.

He'd spent nearly 38% of his income on things he couldn't even specifically remember.

Michael doesn't need a lecture about lattes. He needs a system.

Budgeting has a branding problem.

Say the word "budget" and most people picture spreadsheets, restriction, saying no to everything fun, and generally living like a financial monk. It sounds like a diet—and we all know how well diets work. You white-knuckle it for a few weeks, slip up, feel like a failure, and abandon the whole thing.

No wonder most budgets fail by February.

But a budget isn't a punishment. It's a plan. It's you deciding in advance where your money goes instead of looking back and wondering where it went. Done right, a budget actually gives you *more* freedom—because you're spending intentionally on stuff that matters instead of bleeding money on stuff that doesn't.

The trick is finding a system that works for your actual life. Not some imaginary version of you who never orders DoorDash.

The methods in this chapter are the most popular starting points, but they're not the only options. Plenty of people take pieces from two or three approaches and build something custom. Jordan might start with 50/30/20 for the big-picture framework but use digital envelopes for the categories where she overspends. Michael might run zero-based budgeting for three months to get his spending under control, then switch to pay-yourself-first once the habits stick. There's no rule that says you have to pick one method and follow it exactly. The goal is a system you'll actually use — however you get there.

Why Most Budgets Fail

Before we get into methods, let's talk about why budgeting attempts crash and burn. Understanding the failure points helps you avoid them.

They're too complicated. If your budget requires a finance degree and three hours every Sunday to maintain, you won't maintain it. You don't need 47 categories. You need a system simple enough that you'll use it when you're tired, busy, or not in the mood. Jordan downloaded a budgeting app, set up twenty-two categories, tracked every dollar for nine days, got overwhelmed, and deleted the app. She's not lazy. The system was wrong for her brain.

They're too restrictive. A budget that eliminates all fun is a budget begging to be broken. Humans aren't robots. If your budget makes you feel deprived constantly, you'll eventually snap and blow $300 on something just to feel alive. Sustainability beats perfection. A "pretty good" budget you follow for years beats a "perfect" budget you abandon in six weeks.

They're not based in reality. Tyler's take-home is $1,190 a month. If he budgets $200 for food and consistently spends $290, the budget is wrong—not Tyler. You can't budget for the life you wish you had. You have to budget for the life you actually live, then adjust gradually.

They don't account for real life. Cars break down. Friends get married. Laptops die before finals. Budgets without cushion for the unexpected collapse at the first surprise expense.

The "fresh start" trap. "I'll start over next month." You overspend in week two, decide the month is ruined, mentally check out, and promise you'll do better on the first. But next month, something else happens. A budget isn't pass/fail. It's information. If you go over in one category, you adjust. You don't burn the whole thing down.

Budgeting Methods: Find Your Fit

There's no single right way to budget. Different methods work for different brains. Here are the main approaches—and which of our cast each one fits best.

The 50/30/20 Rule

50% of take-home pay goes to needs (rent, utilities, insurance, minimum debt payments, groceries). **30%** goes to wants (dining out, entertainment, shopping, hobbies). **20%** goes to savings and extra debt payments.

Simple, flexible, and a solid starting point if you've never budgeted before. The problem? It assumes your needs fit in 50%, which is increasingly unrealistic in expensive cities.

Let's see how it maps to our cast:

50/30/20 Applied to Each Character's Take-Home

Estimates based on 2026 figures.

Character	Monthly Take-Home	50% Needs	30% Wants	20% Savings/Debt
Tyler	$1,190	$595	$357	$238
Jordan	$3,200	$1,600	$960	$640
Mia (avg month)	$2,500	$1,250	$750	$500
Michael	$3,550	$1,775	$1,065	$710
Emma	$3,850	$1,925	$1,155	$770

Some of these work on paper. Emma's needs are well under 50%—she's in good shape. Jordan's rent ($875) plus student loan minimums ($380) plus insurance ($180) plus utilities and groceries already hits $1,700—over her $1,600 needs target. Michael's car payment alone ($485) plus rent ($1,200) already eats $1,685 of his $1,775 needs budget, leaving $90 for food, utilities, and insurance.

The fix: If your needs exceed 50%, don't abandon the framework—adjust the ratios. Jordan might run 55/25/20. Michael, while paying down credit card debt, might need 60/15/25 (heavier on needs and debt payments, lighter on wants). Tyler, living at home with minimal fixed costs, could flip it: 30/30/40 and bank the savings advantage while he has it.

The ratios are guidelines, not scripture.

Zero-Based Budgeting

Every dollar of your income gets assigned a job *before* the month starts. Income minus all allocated expenses equals zero. Nothing floats unaccounted for.

This is the method Michael needs. His problem isn't big irresponsible purchases—it's the $1,340 in monthly spending he can't even remember. Zero-based budgeting forces him to decide in advance: this $40 goes to DoorDash, this $50 goes to going out, this $100 goes to random shopping. When the category's spent, it's spent.

Michael's Zero-Based Budget ($3,550 take-home)

Category	Amount
Rent	$1,200
Car payment	$485
Car insurance	$130
Utilities (electric, internet)	$140
Phone	$85
Groceries	$350
Gas	$120
Dining out	$120
Subscriptions (Spotify, streaming)	$25
Fun/personal spending	$100
CC minimum payments	$240
Extra CC payment (avalanche)	$200
Emergency fund building	$150
Sinking fund (car maintenance, haircuts, etc.)	$100
Buffer/miscellaneous	$105
Total	**$3,550**

Every dollar has a destination. Michael's "random spending" drops from $1,340 to $220 (dining out + fun money), but he's not deprived—he chose those numbers. The difference is that $350 a month is now going toward fixing his financial situation instead of disappearing into his transaction history.

Best for: People who need tight control, are paying off debt, or (like Michael) have a spending leak they can't locate. The tradeoff: it takes more setup and weekly maintenance.

Pay Yourself First (The Anti-Budget)

Automate your savings and bill payments first. Whatever's left, spend guilt-free without tracking every purchase.

This is Emma's method. She doesn't have a spending problem—she has an optimization problem. She needs to make sure the right amounts are going to the right places automatically, and then she can stop checking her bank balance every day.

Emma's Pay-Yourself-First Setup

Priority	Destination	Amount	Timing
1	TSP (Roth) contribution	$283 (5%)	Auto from paycheck
2	Emergency fund (HYSA)	$200	Auto-transfer payday
3	Roth IRA	$300	Auto-transfer payday
4	Sinking funds	$150	Auto-transfer payday
5	All bills on autopay	$1,400	Various dates
6	Everything else	$1,517	Spend freely

Emma doesn't need to track whether she spent $32 or $38 on lunch. She needs to know that the important money is moving first. After her automated priorities, whatever's left is hers. No guilt, no spreadsheet.

Best for: People with stable income who don't overspend but struggle to save consistently. Also good for anyone who finds detailed budgeting soul-crushing.

The Envelope System (Modern Version)

Divide your spending money into categories—digital "envelopes"—and when a category is empty, you're done for the month.

Mia uses a version of this for her variable income. Since she doesn't know what she'll earn each month, she can't do a traditional monthly budget. Instead, she operates on a cash-stuffing system with digital envelopes: every time money comes in from a bartending shift or freelance payment, she immediately splits it.

Mia's Variable Income Envelope System

Envelope	Rule
Taxes	30% of every freelance payment (separate savings account)
Rent & bills	$950 set aside first (her share of the 4-way split apartment + utilities)
Groceries & basics	$250/month
Fun	$150/month (when she can afford it)
Savings	Whatever's left after the above

In a $3,500 month, Mia has about $450 left after taxes, rent, food, and fun to put toward savings. In a $2,000 month, she barely covers her essentials and savings gets nothing. That's the reality of variable income—and it's why Mia budgets off her floor ($2,000), not her ceiling ($3,500). Anything above the floor is a bonus that goes to building her cushion.

Best for: Variable income earners, visual thinkers, and people who overspend when money feels abstract. The modern version uses apps like YNAB or Goodbudget, or simply separate bank accounts for each "envelope."

The 80/20 Budget

Save 20% automatically. Spend 80% however you want. No tracking.

That's it. That's the whole system.

Tyler could start here. His financial life is simple enough—he lives at home, has minimal fixed costs, and hasn't accumulated the kind of spending complexity that requires detailed tracking. If he automates $238/month (20% of his $1,190 take-home) into savings and spends the rest, he's building a financial foundation without any effort.

Best for: People with simple finances who want the absolute lowest-effort approach. The weakness: it won't catch lifestyle creep or category problems. But it's infinitely better than no system at all.

Budgeting Method Quick-Match

If you're...	Try this method
New to budgeting, want something simple	50/30/20 or 80/20
Paying off debt aggressively	Zero-based
Earning variable income (gig, freelance, tips)	Envelope system with floor-based budgeting
Already saving but want to optimize	Pay yourself first
Struggling with impulse spending	Zero-based or envelope
Hate tracking every dollar	Pay yourself first or 80/20

Finding What Works for Your Brain

Budgeting methods aren't one-size-fits-all because brains aren't one-size-fits-all.

If you have ADHD or executive function challenges: Keep it simple. Automate everything. Use visual cues—apps with graphs, a whiteboard on your wall, progress bars. Try weekly budgets instead of monthly; shorter time frames are easier to conceptualize. Build in fun money, because deprivation plus impulsivity equals budget disaster.

If you're anxious about money: Don't over-track. Checking your accounts twelve times a day isn't planning—it's ruminating. Set a specific weekly check-in time and try to let it go outside of that window. Automate to reduce the number of decisions you need to make. Build a buffer—even a small one quiets the "what if" voice.

If you're a spender by nature: Use friction. Remove saved payment info from apps. Delete shopping apps from your phone. Wait 24–48 hours before any non-essential purchase over $50. Separate your spending money into a different account than your bills and savings—when it's gone, it's gone. Michael calls this his "stupid money account." It works because it has a limit.

The Roommate Problem (And Other Social Money Awkwardness)

One of the biggest budget-wrecking forces for the 18–28 age group isn't subscriptions or coffee. It's other people.

Splitting rent when it's not equal. Jordan's roommate has the bigger bedroom with the attached bathroom. They split rent 50/50. Jordan knows this isn't fair but hasn't said anything because she doesn't want to be "that person." She's effectively subsidizing her roommate by about $100/month. Over a year, that's $1,200—more than enough to fund a small emergency fund.

The friend who never Venmos back. Tyler spotted a friend $40 for concert tickets three months ago. The friend hasn't mentioned it since. Tyler checks the Venmo request he sent—still pending. He's embarrassed to bring it up, so he just... absorbs the loss. This keeps happening with different friends and different amounts. It adds up.

"Let's split the check evenly." Mia orders a $14 salad and water. Three friends order $30 entrees with drinks. Someone suggests splitting evenly. Mia's share goes from $14 to $32. She can't afford the difference, but saying so feels humiliating. So she pays, and that's $18 she didn't budget for.

The group trip you can't afford. Michael's friends are planning a weekend trip—Airbnb, restaurants, activities. Estimated cost: $400. Michael has $8,000 in credit card debt. He knows he should say no. He goes anyway and puts it on the card.

There's no financial hack for these situations. They require something harder: a conversation. "Hey, can we split rent proportional to room size?" "Hey, can you get me back for those tickets?" "Hey, I'm going to pay for just my meal—is that cool?" "Hey, I can't swing this trip right now."

Every single one of those sentences feels uncomfortable to say. Every single one of them protects your budget.

Tools That Actually Help

A quick note: the personal finance app landscape changes constantly. Apps get acquired, shut down, or change pricing. These were solid options at the time of writing, but the best budgeting system is one you'll actually use—whether it's a cutting-edge app, a spreadsheet, or pen and paper.

Budgeting App Comparison

App	Cost	Best For	Method
YNAB	$14.99/mo ($99/yr; free for students)	Intentional budgeters, debt payoff	Zero-based
Goodbudget	Free (limited) / $10/mo	Couples, visual thinkers	Digital envelopes
EveryDollar	Free (manual) / Premium available	Simple zero-based budgets	Zero-based
Copilot	$10/mo ($70/yr; iOS only)	Hands-off trackers who want good visuals	Automatic tracking
Google Sheets	Free	DIY types, customizers	Whatever you build
Pen and paper	Free	People who think better on paper	Anything

Building Your First Budget: Quick Start

If you've never budgeted before, here's how to start without overthinking it.

Step 1: Know your take-home pay. After taxes and deductions—the actual number that lands in your account. If it varies (Mia), use the average of the last three months or your lowest recent month.

Step 2: List your fixed expenses. Rent, car payment, insurance, phone, subscriptions, minimum debt payments. These are non-negotiable and roughly the same each month.

Step 3: Estimate your variable expenses. Look at the last two or three months of actual spending. How much are you *really* spending on groceries, gas, dining out, entertainment? Don't guess—look at real numbers. Michael's DoorDash reckoning happened because he'd never looked.

Step 4: Subtract from income. If the number is positive, decide where the surplus goes (savings, debt payoff, fun money). If it's negative, you're spending more than you earn. Something has to change—either income goes up or expenses come down.

Step 5: Set one priority goal. Don't try to do everything at once. Pick one: build a $500 emergency fund, pay off a credit card, save for something specific. Direct extra money there.

Step 6: Revisit weekly at first. Check in every week for the first couple months. After a few months, move to monthly check-ins once you know your patterns.

A budget isn't a cage. It's a tool. The goal isn't to restrict your life—it's to make sure your money goes toward stuff that actually matters instead of disappearing into random charges you don't remember making.

Find a system. Keep it simple. Adjust as you go.

When Your Partner Spends Differently (The Harder Conversation)

Emma's been dating Marcus for eleven months. He's kind, funny, works in sales, makes about $52,000. She likes him. She can see a future.

The problem is Tuesday nights.

Tuesday is their standing dinner date. Marcus picks the restaurant—always somewhere new, always $80-120 for two after drinks and tip. Emma suggested cooking at home once. He said sure, then booked a reservation anyway because he'd "already been thinking about this place."

It's not just dinners. It's the weekends away he floats without checking what she has budgeted. It's the $400 concert tickets he buys and says "don't worry about paying me back" in a tone that means she's supposed to offer. It's the Christmas gifts that are generous enough to make her $75 budget feel cheap by comparison.

Emma earns $68,000, contributes 5% to her TSP, has $4,200 in savings, zero debt, and a monthly budget she's followed for two years. Marcus makes $52,000, has $800 in savings, no retirement contributions, and a credit card balance he won't tell her the exact number on. When she asked once, he said "it's handled."

She doesn't think he's irresponsible. She thinks he values experiences and generosity and doesn't want money to dictate how he lives. She respects that—in theory. In practice, she's spending $600-700/month on the relationship, her savings rate has dropped from 15% to 8%, and she's started quietly resenting the restaurant bills she smiles through.

Last week, Marcus brought up moving in together. Split the rent, save money, take the next step. He framed it as the logical move. Emma ran the numbers in her head before he finished the sentence: his $800 in savings means she'd be covering the security deposit, the furniture, and any emergency that hit in the first six months. She'd essentially be the financial safety net for two people on one person's planning.

She said "let's talk about it more" and changed the subject. She hasn't brought it up since.

The Real Problem Under the Surface

Here's what Emma is dealing with—the thing nobody warns you about: financial discipline can become a source of loneliness. She's done everything right. She has the budget, the emergency fund, the retirement contributions. And the reward is sitting across from someone she cares about, doing mental math on the entrée prices while he orders a second cocktail, feeling like the killjoy in a relationship that's supposed to be fun.

This isn't about $80 dinners. It's about whether she's going to spend the next ten years being the adult in a relationship. It's about whether "I love you" includes "I'll build something stable with you" or just "I'll take you out when I feel like it."

She doesn't want to control his money. She wants to know they're building toward the same things. And she doesn't know how to say that without sounding like his mother.

Why Marcus Spends

Marcus grew up in a house where money was tight. Not poverty, but the kind of tight where you notice. His parents fought about bills. Vacations didn't happen. Nice dinners out were reserved for birthdays, and even then, his dad would stress about the cost for days afterward.

Now Marcus makes $52,000. He has a job he's good at. He can take Emma to a nice restaurant on a Tuesday without asking permission or checking his account balance first. That feels like proof—proof that he made it, that he's not his parents, that money doesn't have to be this source of anxiety and restriction.

He doesn't see his spending as reckless. He sees it as freedom. And if Emma makes him budget, if she asks him to track every dollar and plan every expense, she's taking that freedom away. She's turning money back into the thing his parents fought about.

He's not trying to hurt her. He just doesn't see what she sees. To him, the $120 dinner is an investment in their relationship. To her, it's $120 that could've gone toward the security deposit for the apartment they're supposedly building toward together.

They're operating from completely different systems. And neither of them knows how to bridge the gap.

What Emma Knows (And Hasn't Said)

Emma knew what she was supposed to do. She'd tell him they needed to talk. She'd lay out her budget, get his numbers, establish boundaries. She could walk him through it like a financial planner, not a girlfriend.

But that's not what stopped her.

What stopped her was the fear that if she said "we need to have a money talk," what he heard was "I don't think you're good enough." That his generosity—the thing he was proud of, the thing that made him feel like he'd escaped his parents' financial stress—would become the problem. That she'd become the person who made money stressful again.

So she stayed quiet. She smiled through the dinners. She said yes to the weekend trips. She let her savings rate drop from 15% to 8% and told herself it was temporary, that once they moved in together it would balance out.

Except it wouldn't. Because moving in together without this conversation meant she'd be covering his financial gaps while he kept spending like he always had. And the resentment she felt now—the quiet, simmering kind that made her check the menu prices before he even sat down—would turn into something bigger. Something that ended relationships.

That fear was costing her $600 a month.

The Conversation She Finally Had

Emma decided Saturday morning, before Marcus woke up. That's when she'd do it. Not from anger, not mid-dinner, not when a bill arrived. Just... clear.

She ran through what she'd say a dozen times, trying to find words that didn't sound like accusation. That didn't make her sound like his accountant instead of his girlfriend. Finally she landed on something true:

"I need you to understand my money isn't just money to me. It's my safety. And I need to know you see that."

When Marcus woke up, she made coffee and sat down across from him. "I want to talk about money. Not because anything is wrong, but because I care about where this is going and I want us to be honest about it."

She didn't open with his spending. She opened with hers—what she earned, what she saved, what her goals were. She made herself vulnerable first. Then she asked him to do the same. Not a full audit. Just the basics: what do you earn, what do you owe, what are you saving toward?

Marcus got defensive at first. "I told you, it's handled." But Emma didn't back down. "I'm not asking if it's handled. I'm asking what the number is. Because if we're going to move in together, I need to know if we're both starting from the same place."

He told her. $6,400 on two credit cards. No emergency fund. No retirement contributions. He'd been paying minimums and hoping the balance would somehow shrink on its own.

Emma didn't judge. She didn't lecture. She just said, "Okay. Now I know. And now we can figure out what moving in together actually looks like."

They built a plan: a monthly "relationship budget" they both agreed on ($400 for dates and activities—enough to enjoy themselves, not enough to wreck either person's plan), a rule about purchases over $200 getting a heads-up, and an honest timeline for moving in together that included Marcus building his emergency fund to at least $2,000 first.

It wasn't a perfect conversation. Marcus felt embarrassed about the credit card debt. Emma felt guilty for making him feel that way. But they had it. And that changed everything.

What Not to Do

Emma could've led with his spending. She could've opened with "you're spending too much and it's hurting us." The moment she did that, he would've stopped listening and started defending. The conversation would've become about whether he was irresponsible instead of whether they were building toward the same things.

She could've made it about shame. About what he was doing wrong. About how she was the responsible one and he needed to get it together. That would've ended the relationship, not saved it.

She could've stayed silent. Let the resentment build. Smiled through another year of $120 dinners while her savings rate dropped and her frustration grew. Eventually, they would've fought—not about money directly, but about dishes or plans or something small that was really about the credit card bill underneath.

The couples who avoid money conversations don't avoid conflict. They just delay it until it's too late to fix.

Why This Matters

Emma's financial skills aren't a liability. They're an asset. She just had to be willing to share them with someone who hadn't learned the same lessons yet—and patient enough to let him learn.

Marcus isn't a villain. He's someone operating from a different money story. And once Emma understood that—once she stopped seeing his spending as a judgment of her values and started seeing it as a different operating system—the conversation became possible.

The move-in conversation isn't about rent. It's about whether both people have emergency funds, whether both people are saving for retirement, whether one person is going to quietly carry the financial load while the other enjoys the ride. Emma needed to know those answers before she signed a lease with anyone.

The couples who have these conversations early—even awkwardly, even imperfectly—are the ones who last. The ones who avoid them end up fighting about dishes when they're really fighting about the credit card bill underneath.

Money conversations in relationships are hard. But they're not optional. And the earlier you have them, the better your odds.

Your Move

- **Today:** Look at last month's transactions. Find the total you spent on things you can't specifically remember.
- **This week:** Pick one budgeting method from this chapter and try it. Not forever. Just one month.
- **This month:** Set up one automatic transfer—savings, debt payment, anything. Make it small enough to sustain. The automation matters more than the amount.

When It Goes Sideways

"I blew my budget at a music festival."

Tyler saved $300 for a weekend music festival—tickets, food, gas. He budgeted carefully. Then he got there and everything was more expensive than he expected. $8 water bottles. $16 food truck meals. A $45 t-shirt. His friends were buying rounds. By Sunday, he'd spent $580—$280 over budget—and put the difference on a friend's credit card with a promise to pay them back.

Here's the thing about festivals, vacations, and weddings: your normal spending instincts don't apply. You're already there. You've already committed. Saying no in the moment feels like ruining the experience. And the vendors know you're a captive audience—they price accordingly.

So what does Tyler do now? First, pay the friend back immediately. Money owed to friends corrodes relationships faster than interest corrodes debt. Second, stop pretending next time will be different unless he changes the system. Tyler's $300 budget was based on wishful thinking. The real cost of a festival weekend—food, drinks, merch, the stuff you didn't plan for—is closer to $600. So he builds a "festivals and events" sinking fund based on the real number, not the optimistic one. And next time, he brings cash. When the cash is gone, the spending stops. No app, no willpower required—just an empty wallet.

What this isn't: a reason to swear off festivals forever. The financial monk approach doesn't last, and you'll resent the budget that made you stay home. Budget honestly, plan for the real cost, and enjoy it without the guilt hangover

"My roommate owes me money and I don't know what to do."

What happened: Jordan covered her roommate's half of the electric bill two months ago ($95) because her roommate was "between paychecks." Then it happened again with groceries ($60). Jordan has asked once—casually, over text—and got a "yeah I'll get you back soon" response. It's been six weeks. Jordan is now quietly resentful every time her roommate orders takeout.

Why it happens: Money between friends and roommates is uniquely uncomfortable. Asking for money you're owed feels confrontational, even though it's completely reasonable. The person who owes often isn't being malicious—they've mentally downgraded the debt because it wasn't formalized. There was no interest rate, no due date, no consequence for not paying. So it slides.

What to do: Have a direct conversation—not a text. "Hey, I want to clear this up before it becomes a thing. You owe me $155 from the electric bill and groceries. Can you Venmo me by Friday?" If your roommate can't pay it all at once, agree on a payment plan. Going forward, use a shared expense app (Splitwise is free) that tracks who owes what in real time. Establish a rule: shared expenses get settled within a week. Not "soon." Within a week.

What not to do: Let it fester. The longer money owed goes unaddressed, the more it damages the relationship—and the less likely you are to get paid. Also, don't lend money you can't afford to lose. If $95 puts your budget in jeopardy, the answer is "I can't cover your half this month."

"I've quit budgeting three times. I'm not a budget person."

What happened: Michael has downloaded four budgeting apps in the past two years. Each time, he sets it up with enthusiasm, tracks everything for about two weeks, misses a few entries, falls behind, feels guilty, and deletes the app. He's concluded that budgeting isn't for him.

Why it happens: Michael didn't fail at budgeting. He failed at *that particular budgeting method* three or four times. Each attempt was essentially the same approach—detailed tracking of every transaction—which requires sustained daily attention. For someone who drip-spends out of boredom and exhaustion, adding "meticulously log your spending" to the end of every day is asking for failure.

What to do: Try a method that works *with* Michael's brain instead of against it. The pay-yourself-first approach requires ten minutes of setup and then runs on autopilot. Automate $350/month to debt payments and savings the day his paycheck hits. Set all bills to autopay. Whatever's left in his checking account is his to spend without tracking. He doesn't need to know whether he spent $12.47 at Chipotle—he needs to know the important money moved first. If he wants more control later, he can layer in zero-based budgeting once the automation habit is established. But the automation comes first.

What not to do: Conclude you're "bad with money" and stop trying. The budgeting industry has convinced people that if you can't maintain a detailed spending log, you're financially irresponsible. That's like saying if you can't run a marathon, you shouldn't exercise. There are easier ways to move. Find one.

"I can't stop impulse-buying when I scroll."

What happened: Mia bought $187 worth of stuff from Instagram ads in a single week. A skincare set ($48), a phone case ($22), a pair of shoes ($89), and a kitchen gadget ($28). Each purchase felt justified in the moment—the ad made a good case, the reviews were solid, and one-click checkout meant it was done before she finished her coffee. By Friday, she had three packages on her doorstep and a checking account $187 lighter than planned.

Why it happens: Social media advertising is engineered to trigger impulse purchases. The algorithm learns what you pause on, what you click, and what you buy—then serves you more of the same. One-click checkout, saved payment info, and "only 3 left in stock" urgency messages remove every speed bump between desire and purchase. Your brain gets a dopamine hit from the buying, not from the having. That's why the packages often sit unopened.

What to do: Put obstacles between you and the purchase. Remove saved payment info from Instagram and any app where you impulse-buy. Unfollow or mute accounts that are essentially storefronts. Institute a 48-hour rule: screenshot the item, wait two days, and see if you still want it. Most of the time, you won't. For the things you do still want, budget for them—Mia added a $75/month "online shopping" envelope. When it's gone, it's gone. The impulse doesn't disappear, but the spending limit does.

What not to do: Delete all social media. That's an overcorrection most people won't sustain. The goal is awareness and speed bumps, not eliminating the internet. Also, don't return everything in a shame spiral—evaluate each purchase honestly. If you'll use it and it fits your budget, keep it. If it was pure impulse, return it and redirect the refund to savings.

A budget isn't about tracking every penny for the rest of your life. It's about knowing where your money goes so you can send it where you actually want it to go. Michael's $1,340 in untracked spending wasn't a character flaw—it was a system failure. Emma's $600/month in relationship spending wasn't about Marcus—it was about a conversation she hadn't had yet.

The system you pick matters less than whether you use it. Try one. Adjust. Try another. The goal is a budget you'll actually follow on a tired Wednesday night, not one that only works when you're motivated.

Start this week. Imperfect counts.

Chapter 4: Building Your Safety Net

> *"The goal isn't to be rich. The goal is to be able to handle the unexpected without it destroying you." —Tiffany Aliche, The Budgetnista*

Mia's car started making a grinding noise on a Tuesday. By Thursday, the mechanic told her the brakes needed replacing — $1,200 for parts and labor. Non-negotiable. The grinding was metal on metal. Driving the car as-is was dangerous.

Mia had $87 in her savings account. Her checking had $340, and rent was due in nine days.

She did the math sitting in the mechanic's waiting room. She couldn't afford the repair. She couldn't afford *not* to do the repair — the car was how she got to her bartending job, how she drove to freelance client meetings, how she did everything. Without the car, her income drops to zero within a week.

So she put the $1,200 on a credit card she'd been offered in the mail three months earlier. She hadn't planned to use it. The interest rate was 26.99% APR. She signed the receipt, drove home with new brakes, and tried not to think about what she'd just done.

Over the next eight months, making minimum payments of $35, Mia paid $280 in interest before she finally cleared the balance. Her $1,200 brake job cost $1,480. And during those eight months, two more unexpected expenses hit — a $175 urgent care copay and a $90 phone screen replacement — both of which went on the same card.

This is how it starts. One emergency without a cushion. Then another. Then another. The debt stacks. The interest compounds. And a person who was doing fine three months ago is suddenly carrying a balance she can't shake.

An emergency fund would have stopped the whole chain. Not the brakes — those were happening regardless. But the $1,200 would have come from savings instead of a credit card, and the $280 in interest would still be in Mia's pocket.

An emergency fund is boring. Nobody posts about it on Instagram. There's no dopamine hit from watching money sit in a savings account doing nothing.

But it's the difference between "my car broke down, that's annoying" and "my car broke down and now I'm trapped in a debt cycle I can't escape."

What Actually Counts as an Emergency

Let's get clear on this, because "emergency" is a word that gets stretched thin when you want something badly enough.

Emergencies vs. Not Emergencies

Real Emergencies	Not Emergencies (Even If They Feel Urgent)
Job loss or sudden income drop	Concert tickets that just went on sale
Medical bills or unexpected health issues	A really good sale on something you want
Car repairs needed to get to work	Your friend's destination birthday trip
Emergency travel (family crisis, death)	A new phone because yours is two years old
Essential home/apartment repairs (heat dies, pipe bursts)	Holiday gifts you didn't budget for
Necessary replacements (only work shoes fell apart, glasses broke)	"I deserve this" purchases after a hard week

Tyler's test: before touching his emergency fund, he asks himself one question — "If I don't spend this money right now, will something in my life actually break?" New tires when the tread is gone? Yes. New sneakers because his are scuffed? No. That goes in the sinking fund or waits for next month's budget.

How Much Do You Actually Need?

The standard advice is 3–6 months of expenses. That's a good target. It's also completely overwhelming if you're starting from zero.

So let's break it into stages, and see what each one looks like for our cast:

Emergency Fund Stages

Stage	Target	What It Covers
1: Starter Fund	$500–$1,000	A single common emergency: car repair, medical copay, essential replacement
2: One Month	1× monthly essentials	Buys time for a minor income disruption
3: Three Months	3× monthly essentials	Real runway for job loss or major setback
4: Full Safety Net	6× monthly essentials	Weather almost any storm without panic

What Each Stage Looks Like Per Character

Based on each person's bare-bones monthly expenses (rent, utilities, food, transportation, minimum debt payments).

Character	Bare-Bones Monthly	Stage 1	Stage 2	Stage 3	Stage 4
Tyler	$800	$500	$800	$2,400	$4,800
Jordan	$1,700	$1,000	$1,700	$5,100	$10,200
Mia	$1,400	$1,000	$1,400	$4,200	$8,400
Michael	$2,200	$1,000	$2,200	$6,600	$13,200
Emma	$1,800	$1,000	$1,800	$5,400	$10,800

Those Stage 3 and 4 numbers are big. Looking at them can feel impossible, especially when you're starting from $87 like Mia.

That's real. Nobody builds a $10,000 emergency fund in a month. The point of the stages is that each one matters. Tyler's $500 starter fund prevents his next car problem from going on a credit card. That alone changes his financial trajectory.

Should you aim for 3 months or 6?

Lean toward 3 months if you have a stable job with reliable income, marketable skills, low expenses, and other safety nets (family, partner's income, unemployment eligibility). Lean toward 6 months or more if you're self-employed or freelance (Mia), your industry is volatile, you have dependents, you have health issues, or your fixed expenses are high and hard to cut quickly.

Mia, with her variable income and zero employer benefits, needs a bigger cushion than Emma, whose federal job comes with built-in stability, health insurance, and access to unemployment if the worst happens.

Tyler's $500

Tyler opened an account on a Tuesday night.

He was sitting on his bed, still in his warehouse uniform, scrolling through the HYSA options from the list earlier in this chapter. He picked one — Ally, because it was the first name he recognized — and spent twelve minutes filling out the application. Social Security number, checking account link, and a $20 initial transfer.

Twenty dollars. That was it. He stared at the confirmation screen and felt... nothing. Twenty dollars wasn't going to save him from anything. If his car broke down tomorrow, $20 wouldn't cover the tow.

He almost closed the app. But he set up the automatic transfer anyway: $20 every Friday, checking to savings, recurring. Then he put his phone down and went to make dinner.

He didn't think about it for three weeks. The transfers happened in the background. He didn't notice the money missing from his checking account. He didn't notice it accumulating in savings. It was just... running.

Week four, he checked. $80.

Still nothing. Eighty dollars was a tank of gas and some fast food. He closed the app.

Week eight, he checked again because he was bored. $160. A voice in his head said: *that could be a new pair of Jordans.* He closed the app faster this time.

Week twelve: $240. His coworker's car got towed and the guy had to borrow $200 from his mom because he didn't have it. Tyler looked at his $240 and realized: he had it. If that happened to him, he could handle it without calling anyone. That thought landed differently than he expected.

Week sixteen: $320. His friend asked him to split concert tickets — $180 each. Tyler almost pulled from savings. He opened the app, stared at the balance, and thought about his coworker borrowing money from his mom. He texted back: "Can't swing it this month." His friend said "no worries" and that was it. Nobody died. The world kept turning.

Week twenty: $400. Tyler's check engine light came on. His stomach dropped. He took the car to a mechanic who said it was a loose gas cap. No charge. But sitting in that waiting room, Tyler realized something: he wasn't panicking. The old Tyler — the one with $0 in savings — would've spent the whole drive to the mechanic doing math in his head, figuring out which friend to ask for money. This Tyler just... drove there. Because if it was $400, he had $400.

The check engine light wasn't the emergency. But the feeling in that waiting room was the whole point.

Week twenty-five: $500.

Tyler didn't celebrate. He didn't post about it. He just looked at the number and felt something he'd never felt about money before: safe. Not rich. Not comfortable. Just... safe. Like there was a thin wall between him and disaster, and he'd built it himself, $20 at a time.

His mom had never had $500 saved. Not once in his entire childhood. He knew because he'd heard the phone calls — the ones where she whispered to her sister about the electric bill, or asked his grandmother for $200 to cover something that had come due. Those calls were the soundtrack of his childhood, and they'd taught him, without anyone saying it directly, that money was something that happened *to* you. Not something you controlled.

He was eighteen years old, making $16,800 a year at a warehouse, and he had $500 in a savings account that nobody could touch. It had taken six months. Twenty dollars a week. One automated transfer he'd set up in twelve minutes on a Tuesday night.

Tyler's $500 Starter Fund Timeline

Week	Weekly Transfer	Running Total
4	$20	$80
8	$20	$160
12	$20	$240
16	$20	$320
20	$20	$400
25	$20	$500

The table looks simple. It is simple. That's the point.

The amount matters less than the habit. $10 a week gets to $500 in a year. $50 a week gets there in ten weeks. The number you can sustain consistently beats the number you can manage once and then quit. But the table doesn't capture what actually changes. What changes is the feeling in the mechanic's waiting room. The text you send saying "can't swing it" without shame. The quiet knowledge that if something breaks, you're not broken with it.

That's what $500 buys. Not stuff. Options.

Where to Keep It

Your emergency fund needs to be accessible (you can get to it quickly) and separate (it's not mixed in with your spending money).

High-Yield Savings Account (HYSA)

A regular savings account at a big bank pays around 0.01% interest — essentially nothing. A high-yield savings account at an online bank pays significantly more, often 3–4% APY depending on the Federal Reserve's interest rate environment.

The Difference on a $5,000 Emergency Fund

Account Type	APY	Annual Interest Earned
Traditional savings (big bank)	0.01%	$0.50
High-yield savings (online bank)	4.00%	$200.00

Same money. Same accessibility. $199.50 difference.

Emma moved her $4,000 savings from her brick-and-mortar bank to an online HYSA after reading an article about it. Took her twenty minutes to open the account and initiate the transfer. She earned more interest in the first month than she'd earned in the previous two years at her old bank.

What to look for in a HYSA: No monthly fees, no minimum balance requirements (or low ones), FDIC insured (up to $250,000 protected), fast transfer times (1–2 business days max), and a decent mobile app. Popular options include Marcus by Goldman Sachs, Ally Bank, Discover Savings, Capital One 360, American Express Savings, and SoFi Savings. These are online banks, which is why they can offer better rates — less overhead than physical branches.

Keep It at a Different Bank

This sounds like extra hassle, but there's a reason: psychological separation. When your emergency fund sits next to your everyday money, transferring it takes two clicks. "I'll just borrow from it this once" becomes a habit.

A separate bank creates friction. You can still access it within a day or two, but there's just enough delay to make you pause and ask whether this is actually an emergency. That pause has saved Jordan from raiding her savings for a "really good deal" on two separate occasions.

Don't Invest Your Emergency Fund

Investments go up and down. The stock market could drop 30% right when you lose your job and need that money. Your $10,000 emergency fund is suddenly $7,000 — exactly when you need every dollar.

Emergency funds stay in cash. Boring? Yes. Safe? Also yes. That's the point.

And no, you can't invest it in crypto. Or meme stocks. Or whatever your friend's cousin is pitching. An emergency fund that's down 40% when your transmission dies isn't an emergency fund. Boring savings account. That's it.

How to Build It When You're Barely Getting By

"Cool, save $1,000. But I have like $47 left at the end of the month."

Fair. Building an emergency fund when money is tight feels impossible. But there's a difference between difficult and impossible.

Automate it. If you have to manually transfer money, you'll find reasons not to — or just forget. Set up an automatic transfer from checking to savings right after payday. Money you never see is money you don't miss as much. Tyler's $20/week doesn't require willpower — it requires a one-time setup.

Cut one thing temporarily. You don't have to overhaul your life. Find one expense you can reduce for a few months and redirect that money. Pause a subscription ($15/month). Cook more, order less ($50–$100/month). Skip the coffee shop for a month ($30–$60/month). This isn't forever — it's a focused sprint.

Use windfalls wisely. Tax refund, birthday money, work bonus, selling stuff you don't need. When unexpected money shows up, don't blow it all, but don't be a robot about it either. A reasonable split: half to the emergency fund, a quarter to debt (if applicable), and a quarter to something you actually want. You're making progress *and* living your life.

Start before you're "ready." There will always be a reason to delay. The perfect time to start saving doesn't exist. Even $20 a month — $240 a year — is infinitely better than $0 and changes your relationship with money in ways that go beyond the dollar amount.

When to Use It (And How to Rebuild)

Emergency funds are meant to be used. Some people build one and then feel so protective of it that they put the car repair on a credit card and pay interest for months to "preserve" their savings. That's backwards. The whole point is to avoid debt when emergencies happen.

Use it when: you're facing a genuine emergency, you've considered other options, and not using it would mean going into debt or missing essential obligations. Don't agonize. Don't feel guilty. This is what the money is for.

Don't use it when: it's something you could have planned for (annual expenses, holidays), you just really want something, you're bailing out someone else's non-emergency, or there are realistic alternatives (adjusting budget, delaying a purchase, payment plan for non-urgent expenses).

How to rebuild after using it: Don't panic — the fund did its job. Pause or reduce other financial goals temporarily (extra debt payments, investing) until you have at least a starter fund again. Same strategy as before: automate, use windfalls, cut temporarily. You've done it once. You can do it again.

If You Lose Your Job: A Quick Action Plan

Job loss is the main reason emergency funds exist. If it happens, here's the playbook:

Week One: Secure the Basics

File for unemployment if you're eligible — and eligibility depends on how you lost the job. If you were laid off or let go without cause, you almost certainly qualify. If you were fired for cause (misconduct, policy violations), your state may deny the claim — though it's still worth filing, since "cause" is narrowly defined and many terminations don't meet the threshold. If you quit voluntarily, you generally don't qualify unless you can demonstrate "good cause" (unsafe working conditions, significant pay cuts, harassment). Rules vary by state, so check your state's unemployment office website for specifics.

Don't wait to file. There's often a waiting period before benefits start, so the sooner you apply, the sooner money arrives. Benefits typically replace 40–50% of your previous income, up to a state maximum. Not enough to live on comfortably, but it stretches your emergency fund significantly.

Assess your health insurance. If you had coverage through your employer, it usually ends at the end of the month you were terminated. Your options depend on *how* you lost the job:

COBRA is available whether you were laid off, fired, or quit — it lets you continue your employer's plan for up to 18 months, but you pay the full premium (your share plus what your employer was paying), often $500–$700+/month. Expensive, but it keeps your same doctors and network.

ACA Marketplace (healthcare.gov) is triggered by an involuntary loss of coverage — layoffs, termination, or losing eligibility. Quitting your job also qualifies as long as you lose your employer-sponsored coverage as a result. You get a 60-day Special Enrollment Period. Depending on your new (lower) income, subsidies can make this significantly cheaper than COBRA.

Medicaid kicks in based on income, not how you lost your job. If your income drops low enough — and the threshold varies by state — you may qualify for free or very low-cost coverage regardless of whether you were laid off or walked out the door.

Short-term health insurance is a stopgap anyone can buy, but read the fine print — these plans often don't cover pre-existing conditions or many essential services. Better than nothing, not a long-term solution.

Emma has an advantage here: as a federal employee, her FEHB coverage would continue through the end of the pay period, and she'd have 31 days to elect temporary continuation. Federal employees also have access to different separation rules than private-sector workers. If you're federal or military, your HR office has specific guidance — use it.

Month One: Stabilize and Plan

Cut to bare-bones spending. Cancel non-essential subscriptions. Review every expense. Your emergency fund needs to stretch.

Reach out to your network. Many jobs are found through connections, not applications. Update LinkedIn, contact former colleagues, tell friends and family. Apply for assistance if needed — SNAP, utility assistance programs, local food banks. There's no shame in using resources that exist for exactly this situation.

Don't touch retirement accounts if you can avoid it. Early withdrawals from a 401(k) or TSP come with taxes plus a 10% penalty. It should be a last resort.

The Math That Shows Why Emergency Funds Are So Powerful

If Jordan loses her job with 3 months of expenses saved ($5,100) and gets unemployment at 40% of her previous income:

	Monthly Amount
Previous take-home	$3,200
Bare-bones expenses	$1,700
Unemployment benefit (40% of gross)	$1,600
Monthly gap to cover from savings	$100
Emergency fund	$5,100
Actual runway	**51 months**

Jordan's 3-month emergency fund, combined with unemployment, stretches her runway well beyond three months. During the first 26 weeks (the typical maximum for unemployment benefits), she's only drawing $100/month from savings — meaning her $5,100 fund barely gets touched. If she hasn't found work by the time unemployment runs out, she still has most of her emergency fund intact to cover the gap. That's the real power of the combination: unemployment covers the early months, and the emergency fund is still there if the search takes longer than expected.

An emergency fund won't make you rich. It won't go viral. It's not exciting.

But it'll let you sleep better. It'll give you options when things go wrong. It'll keep a bad month from becoming a bad year.

Build the cushion. Start now. Start small if you have to.

Your Move

- **Today:** Open a high-yield savings account if you don't have one. It takes 10–15 minutes.
- **This week:** Set up an automatic weekly transfer. Even $10. The habit matters more than the amount.

- **This month:** Calculate your bare-bones monthly expenses. That number times three is your Stage 3 target. Write it down.

When It Goes Sideways

"I used my emergency fund for concert tickets."

What happened: Tyler had been building his emergency fund for four months — $320 saved. His favorite artist announced a surprise tour date in his city. Tickets were $180 and selling fast. His friends were all going. He told himself he'd replace the money next paycheck and transferred $180 out of savings. He didn't replace it next paycheck. Three weeks later, his car needed a $400 tire replacement. He had $140 in savings and put the rest on a friend's credit card.

Why it happens: When you're nineteen and you've never had savings before, $320 doesn't feel like a safety net — it feels like $320 sitting there doing nothing while your friends are buying tickets. The emergency fund is protecting against something that *might* happen. The concert is happening *now*. The present almost always wins over the hypothetical future, especially when social pressure is involved.

What to do: Accept that this happened and don't spiral. Pay your friend back as fast as possible. Then rebuild — and this time, set up a separate sinking fund for entertainment and events. The problem wasn't that Tyler wanted to go to the concert. The problem was that he had no system for fun spending, so the emergency fund became the default source. If he has $50/month going to an "events" fund alongside his emergency savings, the two don't compete.

What not to do: Decide that saving is pointless because you're "just going to spend it anyway." That's the all-or-nothing trap. Tyler saved $320 in four months, which is real progress. He made one mistake. The solution is a better system, not abandoning the habit.

"I can't save anything. I've tried."

What happened: Mia makes \$2,000–\$3,500 a month with no consistency. In her lean months, every dollar goes to rent, food, gas, and utilities. There's nothing left. She's tried saving and the money always gets pulled back out within weeks for something unavoidable.

Why it happens: Variable income makes traditional saving strategies feel impossible — and in the leanest months, they might actually be impossible. Mia isn't failing at saving. She's trying to save on an income that doesn't always cover the basics. That's a math problem, not a discipline problem.

What to do: Separate the strategy for lean months from the strategy for good months. In a \$2,000 month, Mia's only job is to cover her essentials and not go into debt. Saving \$0 in a lean month is not a failure — it's survival, and survival counts. In a \$3,500 month, she has roughly \$1,000 above her baseline. That's where the saving happens. If she puts \$500 of that surplus into emergency savings every good month, and she has six good months a year, that's \$3,000 — more than two months of bare-bones expenses. The key is treating good months as the savings engine, not expecting every month to contribute equally.

What not to do: Beat yourself up during lean months. The instinct to feel like a failure when you can't save is powerful, but it misreads the situation. You're not failing to save — you're succeeding at not going into debt on a tight month. That matters. Also, don't give up on the whole concept because the standard "save X% every month" advice doesn't fit your reality. Build a system that works for variable income, not one designed for a steady paycheck.

“My family keeps asking me for money.”

What happened: Emma’s younger brother calls every couple of months asking to borrow money — $200 here, $150 there. He always says he’ll pay it back. He rarely does. Emma has given him roughly $900 over the past year. She loves her brother and knows he’s struggling, but she’s also watching her own savings stall because she keeps siphoning money to cover his shortfalls.

Why it happens: Family financial pressure is one of the hardest dynamics to navigate, especially in families where the person who’s “doing well” is expected to help everyone else. Emma makes $68,000 — in her family, that makes her the financially stable one. The requests feel small individually, but they add up. And the guilt of saying no to family is heavier than the guilt of saying no to yourself.

What to do: Set a boundary with a specific number. Emma decides she can afford $100/month to help family. She tells her brother: “I want to help, but I have to take care of my own finances too. I can do $100 a month — that’s what I can sustain.” Then she sticks to it. If he asks for more, the answer is “I’ve already hit my limit this month.” She can also help in non-monetary ways: helping him build a budget, reviewing his expenses, connecting him with resources. Sometimes the most loving thing is to teach someone to fish instead of handing them yours.

What not to do: Give until you’re broke. You can’t pour from an empty cup, and sacrificing your own financial stability to fund someone else’s recurring shortfalls helps nobody long-term. Also, don’t lend money you can’t afford to lose — if you “lend” $200 and there’s a good chance it won’t come back, call it a gift in your head and budget accordingly. It saves the relationship and your expectations.

Tyler’s $500 didn’t make him rich. It didn’t even make him comfortable. But it changed something that no spreadsheet can capture: the feeling of knowing that if something breaks, he’s not broken with it. That shift—from fragile to just slightly less fragile—is worth more than the dollar amount.

Mia's emergency fund isn't growing every month. Some months it can't. That's not failure. That's a variable income doing what variable incomes do. The months it grows make up for the months it doesn't.

Build the cushion. Start now. Start small if you have to. The amount matters less than the fact that it exists.

Chapter 5: Debt — The Good, the Bad, and the Crushing

> *"I had assumed if you were going to have fun and do cool things, you almost had to go into debt." —Erin Lowry, Broke Millennial*

Michael knew exactly when his credit card debt stopped being manageable. It wasn't the first charge — that was a legitimate car repair, $740, back when his credit limit was $2,000 and the balance felt temporary. It wasn't the second or third charge, either. Those were groceries and gas during a stretch when his checking account was running low.

It was the Tuesday night in November when he ordered $34 worth of Thai food on DoorDash, watched the pending charge push his balance past $6,000, and closed the app without looking at it again. He didn't do the math. He didn't check his interest rate. He just... kept going. By the time he sat down to actually face the numbers — six months later, after the minimum payments and the compounding interest and a few more "I'll deal with it later" charges — the balance was $8,000 and the minimum payment was barely covering the monthly interest.

Michael doesn't have a spending addiction. He has a debt he stopped paying attention to, and eight months of compound interest did the rest.

Not all debt is created equal.

A mortgage and a maxed-out credit card are completely different animals. One is a strategic tool that can build wealth over time. The other is a trap that keeps you running in place — or sliding backward.

The problem is, nobody explains the difference. Debt is either demonized completely ("never borrow anything ever!") or normalized to the point where drowning in it seems like part of being an adult ("everyone has credit card debt, it's fine").

Neither extreme is useful. Some debt can work for you. Some will work against you. Knowing the difference is one of the most important financial skills you can develop.

How Debt Actually Works

Before we rank the types, let's make sure the mechanics are clear. Debt isn't just "money you owe." It's money that grows.

Principal is the amount you borrowed. **Interest** is the cost of borrowing – what the lender charges for letting you use their money now instead of waiting until you have your own.

With most debt, especially credit cards, interest **compounds**. You pay interest on your interest. This is the same force that makes investing powerful – except now it's working against you.

Here's what that looks like with Michael's situation:

$8,000 Credit Card Debt at 24.99% APR: Payment Scenarios

Strategy	Monthly Payment	Time to Pay Off	Total Interest Paid	Total Cost
Minimum only	$160 (decreasing)	30+ years	$15,500+	$23,500+
Fixed $200/month	$200	7 years, 3 months	$9,334	$17,334
Fixed $400/month	$400	2 years, 3 months	$2,110	$10,110
Fixed $600/month	$600	1 year, 4 months	$1,340	$9,340

At minimum payments, Michael's $8,000 becomes over $23,000. That's not a typo. He'd pay nearly three times what he borrowed, and he'd be making payments into his fifties.

At $400/month — a stretch on his budget, but doable if he cuts back — he's free in just over two years and saves over $13,000 in interest compared to the minimum.

This is why minimum payments are a trap. They're designed to keep you in debt as long as possible while maximizing how much interest you pay.

APR: The Number That Matters

APR stands for Annual Percentage Rate — the yearly interest rate on your balance. Here's how different types of debt compare:

Debt APR Comparison

Debt Type	Typical APR Range	How It Feels
Credit cards	18–29%	Actively painful
Payday loans	300–400%+	Predatory
Buy Now, Pay Later	0–30%	Sneaky
Personal loans	8–20%	Depends on credit
Car loans	5–12%	Manageable if short-term
Federal student loans	5–8%	Slow burn
Private student loans	4–14%	Variable, can spike
Mortgages	6–8%	Historically "good" debt

The higher the APR, the faster your debt grows and the more urgent it is to pay off. Michael's 24.99% credit card should be on fire in his mind. Jordan's 5.5% federal student loans? Those sting, but they're not the emergency.

Types of Debt: Ranked

Potentially Strategic Debt

This is debt that, when used wisely, can help you build wealth or achieve something you couldn't otherwise. The key words are "when used wisely." Every type of strategic debt becomes crushing debt if you overextend.

Mortgage: Borrowing to buy a home can be a wealth-building move — you build equity instead of paying rent that goes nowhere, and real estate generally appreciates over time. But only if you buy within your means, stay long enough to offset closing costs (usually 5+ years), and don't treat your home like an ATM. A mortgage that eats 50% of your income isn't strategic — it's a trap.

Student loans (with major caveats): Borrowing for education can increase your earning potential, but the equation has gotten brutal. Tuition has skyrocketed while entry-level salaries haven't kept pace.

Jordan borrowed $34,000 for her marketing degree. Her starting salary is $48,000. By the salary rule of thumb — keep total debt below your expected first-year salary — she's in reasonable shape. Someone who borrows $120,000 for a degree that leads to a $40,000 job? That math doesn't work, and no amount of optimism changes it.

The salary rule of thumb for student loans: Total borrowing should stay below your expected first-year salary after graduation. This keeps monthly payments at roughly 10% of income on a standard 10-year plan.

Questions to ask before borrowing for school:

Is a state school or community college an option? For many careers, where you went matters far less than that you have the degree. Can you reduce what you borrow by living at home, getting roommates, or working part-time? Is this major likely to lead to a salary that justifies the debt? Are you borrowing federal or private? Always max out federal loans first — they have income-driven repayment and forgiveness programs that private loans don't.

The hard truth: Student loans generally can't be discharged in bankruptcy. This debt follows you. A 22-year-old borrowing $80,000 might not fully grasp that they could still be paying at 35.

Business loans: Borrowing to start or grow a business that generates income can make sense — you're using debt to create something that produces money. But most businesses fail. High-risk debt that only makes sense with a solid plan and realistic projections.

Proceed with Caution Debt

Car loans: You might need a car to get to work. That's real. But cars are depreciating assets — they lose value the moment you drive off the lot and keep losing value every year. We'll go deeper on cars in Chapter 9, including Michael's underwater car situation. For now, the guidelines: buy reliable and used (2–3 years old, certified pre-owned), keep loan terms to 4 years or less, and keep total monthly car costs (payment + insurance + gas + maintenance) under 15–20% of your take-home pay.

Personal loans: Rates are typically lower than credit cards, so they can make sense for consolidating high-interest debt. The danger: paying off credit cards with a personal loan, then running the cards back up. Now you have both.

Bad Debt (Avoid If Possible)

Credit cards (carried balances): Paid off monthly, credit cards are just a convenient payment method that builds credit and earns rewards. Carrying a balance is where they become a trap. At 20%+ APR, the debt grows fast and compounds brutally. The average American with credit card debt owes over $7,000. At minimum payments, that's 15+ years and thousands in interest.

The statement balance rule: To avoid interest charges, pay your *last statement balance* by the due date — not your current balance. Your statement balance is the amount from your previous billing cycle. Pay that in full and you owe zero interest. Pay less, and interest kicks in on the remainder.

Buy Now, Pay Later (BNPL): Klarna, Afterpay, Affirm — these services split purchases into installments, often interest-free if you pay on time. Sounds fine. Here's the problem:

Why BNPL Is Designed to Make You Spend More

The Promise	The Reality
"Split it into 4 easy payments!"	You buy things you can't actually afford
"Interest-free!"	Miss a payment and fees/interest hit hard
"No credit check!"	Multiple BNPL accounts get confusing fast
"Smart shopping!"	Retailers offer it because it increases their sales 20–40%

Mia had three active BNPL plans running at the same time last fall — $35/month to Klarna, $22/month to Afterpay, and $48/month to Affirm. Each individual payment seemed small. Together, that's $105/month in installment payments on things she bought months ago and barely remembers. She was spending current income to pay for past purchases while using BNPL to fund new ones. That's a debt cycle with better marketing.

BNPL services are now starting to report to credit bureaus, so missed payments can damage your score. And some services (Affirm in particular) charge up to 30% APR on longer-term purchases. Read the fine print.

The bottom line on BNPL: If you can't afford to buy something outright, splitting it into four payments doesn't make you able to afford it. It delays the pain while adding risk.

Payday loans: Absolute last resort. These target people in desperate situations and charge astronomical rates — often 400%+ APR when annualized. A $500 payday loan might require $575 back in two weeks. Miss the payment and it rolls over with more fees. This is predatory lending designed to trap people in debt cycles. If you're considering a payday loan, pursue literally any other option first.

Medical Debt: Different Rules

Medical debt plays by different rules than other debt, and most people don't know this.

Medical bills are negotiable. Hospitals charge inflated rates and expect to negotiate. Before paying a large medical bill: request an itemized bill (errors are common), ask about financial assistance (most nonprofit hospitals have charity care programs), negotiate the amount (offering a lump sum often gets a discount), and ask for a payment plan (most providers offer interest-free plans).

Medical debt and credit reporting: As of 2023, medical debt under $500 no longer appears on credit reports. Paid medical debt is also removed. Medical debt can't appear on your credit report until it's been in collections for at least one year — giving you time to resolve it.

Never put medical debt on a credit card unless you can pay it off immediately. Once it's on the card, you lose all negotiating power and start accruing high interest.

Jordan's Student Loans: A Deeper Dive

Jordan owes $34,000 in federal student loans at 5.5% interest. Her standard monthly payment is $380 over 10 years. On her $48,000 salary with $3,200 take-home, that $380 is a real bite — nearly 12% of her take-home pay.

She has options.

Federal vs. Private Loans

This distinction matters enormously. Jordan's loans are all federal, which means she has access to income-driven repayment, deferment, forbearance, and forgiveness programs that private loans don't offer.

Federal vs. Private Student Loans

Feature	Federal	Private
Interest rate	Fixed	Often variable (can increase)

Feature	Federal	Private
Income-driven repayment	Yes	No
Forgiveness programs (PSLF, etc.)	Yes	No
Deferment/forbearance options	Flexible	Limited
Bankruptcy discharge	Extremely rare	Extremely rare
Refinancing risk	Lose federal protections	N/A

Critical rule: Never refinance federal loans into private ones without understanding what you're giving up. The lower rate might look attractive, but you're trading away income-driven repayment, forgiveness eligibility, and flexible hardship options.

Income-Driven Repayment Plans

If Jordan's $380/month is unmanageable, income-driven repayment (IDR) caps her payment at a percentage of her discretionary income:

IDR Plan Comparison

Plan	Payment	Forgiveness After	Best For
SAVE	5% of discretionary income (undergrad)	20 years	Most borrowers; lowest payments
PAYE	10% of discretionary income	20 years	Borrowers after 2007 with high debt-to-income
IBR	10–15% of discretionary income	20–25 years	Borrowers who don't qualify for PAYE
ICR	20% of discretionary income	25 years	Parent PLUS borrowers (after consolidation)

On the SAVE plan, Jordan's estimated payment drops to about $150/month. That's $230/month back in her budget. The tradeoff: she pays more total interest over time, and the forgiveness timeline is 20 years instead of 10. But if cash flow is the immediate problem, IDR gives her room to breathe.

Important IDR notes: You must recertify your income annually — miss this and your payment can spike. Forgiven amounts may be taxable as income (though the SAVE plan has some protections). And IDR means your balance may grow if payments don't cover the interest.

Public Service Loan Forgiveness (PSLF)

Work for a qualifying employer (government, nonprofit, military) and make 120 qualifying monthly payments — that's 10 years — and your remaining federal loan balance is forgiven, tax-free.

Emma qualifies. As a federal GS-9 employee, she's already at a qualifying employer. If she has federal student loans and gets on an IDR plan, every monthly payment counts toward the 120. After 10 years of public service, whatever's left gets wiped clean.

PSLF tips: Submit the Employment Certification Form annually — don't wait until year 10. Use the PSLF Help Tool at studentaid.gov. Make sure you're on an IDR plan. Keep records of everything.

Federal Student Loan Repayment Program (SLRP)

Here's one most people don't know about: federal agencies can repay your student loans as a recruitment or retention incentive — up to $10,000 per year, with a lifetime maximum of $60,000. You must agree to stay with the agency for at least 3 years, and the payments are taxable income. Not all agencies participate, but it's worth asking about during the hiring process. Check job postings for "student loan repayment" as a listed benefit.

Emma should ask her HR office whether her agency offers SLRP. Between PSLF and potential SLRP benefits, her federal employment could be worth tens of thousands in student loan relief.

Michael's Credit Card Debt: The Payoff Plan

Michael owes $8,000 across two cards:

Michael's Debt Snapshot

Card	Balance	APR	Minimum Payment
Card A (Visa)	$5,800	24.99%	$116
Card B (store card)	$2,200	19.99%	$44
Total	**$8,000**		**$160/month**

He has two main strategies:

Avalanche Method: Pay minimums on everything, throw every extra dollar at Card A (highest rate). Mathematically optimal — saves the most interest.

Snowball Method: Pay minimums on everything, throw every extra dollar at Card B (smallest balance). Gets a quick win when that card hits zero, which builds momentum.

Michael's Avalanche Plan ($400/month total)

Month	Card A Balance	Card B Balance	Total Remaining
0	$5,800	$2,200	$8,000
6	$4,313	$2,154	$6,467
12	$2,631	$2,103	$4,734
18	$727	$2,047	$2,774
24	$0	$899	$899
27	$0	$0	$0

Card B barely shrinks while Michael hammers Card A — the $44 minimum mostly covers interest. Once Card A is gone at month 21, the full $400 hits Card B and wipes it out fast.

At $400/month, Michael is debt-free in just over two years. That $400 comes from his zero-based budget in Chapter 3: $240 in minimums plus $160 redirected from the spending he wasn't tracking.

Other Leverage

Balance transfer cards: Some cards offer 0% APR on transfers for 12–21 months. Transfer high-interest debt, pay it down without interest accumulating. The catch: you need good credit (670+) to qualify, there's usually a 3–5% transfer fee, and the post-promotional rate is often 20–29%. Only works if you aggressively pay during the 0% window and don't run up new charges.

Rate negotiation: Call your credit card company and ask for a lower rate. Here's a script that works:

> *"Hi, I've been a customer for [X years] and my current interest rate is [current rate]%. I've been making my payments on time and I'd like to continue being a customer, but I'm considering transferring my balance to a card with a lower rate. Is there anything you can do to lower my APR?"*

If they say no, ask to speak with a supervisor or a retention specialist. If they still say no, call back in a month—you often get a different answer from a different rep. Worst case: they say no. Best case: they drop it a few points. Takes ten minutes.

When to Get Help

Sometimes the hole is too deep to dig out alone. That's not failure — it's reality.

Nonprofit credit counseling (look for agencies affiliated with the National Foundation for Credit Counseling) can help you create a budget, negotiate with creditors, and set up a Debt Management Plan with lower rates. Initial consultations are usually free. **Avoid** for-profit "debt settlement" companies that charge upfront fees and promise to settle for pennies on the dollar. Many are scams.

Signs you need professional help: You can't make minimum payments. You're using one card to pay another. You're considering payday loans. Collectors are calling. You've tried on your own and can't make progress.

Your Rights with Debt Collectors

If debt goes to collections, know your rights under the Fair Debt Collection Practices Act:

What Collectors Cannot Do vs. What You Can Do

They Cannot	You Can
Call before 8 AM or after 9 PM	Request debt validation in writing (within 30 days)
Use threats, profanity, or harassment	Dispute the debt if something is wrong
Lie about what you owe or who they are	Negotiate — they often bought it for pennies on the dollar
Contact you after written cease request	Request "pay for delete" (removal from credit report for payment)
Discuss your debt with family, friends, employers	Send everything certified mail and keep copies

If a collector contacts you, send a validation letter within 30 days. This forces them to prove the debt is real and that they have the right to collect it. Here's what to send (certified mail, always):

Re: Account Number [from their letter]

I am requesting validation of this debt under the Fair Debt Collection Practices Act. Please provide: the amount of the debt and how it was calculated, the name of the original creditor, proof that you are authorized to collect this debt, and proof that the statute of limitations has not expired. I do not acknowledge this debt. Do not contact me further until you have provided the requested validation.

Until they validate, they cannot legally continue collection activity. Michael used this approach with his medical collection in Chapter 6—it works.

The statute of limitations matters: Every state has a time limit on how long a creditor can sue you — usually 3–6 years. After that, the debt is "time-barred." Collectors can still try to collect, but they can't sue. Making a payment or acknowledging the debt in writing can restart the clock. Be careful what you say or sign.

Bankruptcy: Not a Life Sentence

Bankruptcy exists for a reason. It's a legal tool, not a moral failing.

Chapter 7 wipes out most unsecured debt (credit cards, medical bills, personal loans). You may lose some assets, but most people keep most of their stuff through exemptions. Retirement accounts (401(k), TSP, IRA) are fully protected. Stays on credit for 10 years, but impact diminishes over time.

Chapter 13 creates a 3–5 year court-supervised repayment plan. Better if you have too much income for Chapter 7 or want to catch up on mortgage/car payments. Stays on credit for 7 years.

When to consider it: Your unsecured debt exceeds half your annual income. You couldn't pay it off in 5 years even with aggressive budgeting. You're facing lawsuits or wage garnishment. You've tried other options and can't make progress.

Many people see credit scores above 700 within 2–3 years of bankruptcy. It's not the end. If you're considering it, consult a bankruptcy attorney — many offer free consultations.

Debt can feel permanent. It's not.

People dig out of $50,000, $100,000, even more. It takes time, honesty about what you're dealing with, and a plan you actually follow.

One payment at a time.

Your Move

- **Today:** List every debt you have: balance, interest rate, minimum payment. All of them. On one page.
- **This week:** Pick avalanche or snowball. Set up the extra payment on your target debt.
- **This month:** Call one credit card company and ask for a lower rate. Use the script in this chapter. Ten minutes, potential savings of hundreds.

When It Goes Sideways

"I've been paying minimums for two years and the balance barely moved."

What happened: Michael made minimum payments on his Visa for two years. He paid $116/month, every month, on time. He felt responsible. Then he checked his balance and realized it had only dropped from $5,800 to $5,100. Two years of payments — $2,784 total — and only $700 went to principal. The rest was interest.

Why it happens: At 24.99% APR, Michael's card accrues about $120 in interest per month on a $5,800 balance. His minimum payment of $116 doesn't even cover the monthly interest. The balance is technically growing, and the minimum payment is just slowing the growth. This is by design. Credit card companies set minimums low enough to keep you in debt for decades while maximizing their revenue.

What to do: Any amount above the minimum goes directly to principal. Even $50 extra per month changes the math dramatically. Michael's zero-based budget from Chapter 3 freed up $160 beyond his minimums. That $160 goes straight to the highest-rate card. If he can't find extra money in the budget, look at the income side: pick up overtime, sell things, do a side hustle for three months. Treat it like a sprint, not a marathon. The goal is to get the balance below the tipping point where payments actually outpace interest.

What not to do: Keep paying minimums and assume you're making progress. You're not. Also, don't close the card once it's paid off — that hurts your credit utilization ratio. Pay it off, cut it up if you need to, but leave the account open.

"I owe my friend money and it's ruining the friendship."

Tyler borrowed $300 from a friend four months ago when his car needed an unexpected repair and he hadn't built his emergency fund yet. He said he'd pay it back in two weeks.

It's been four months. He's avoided his friend's texts. Skipped a group hangout because he didn't want the awkwardness. He can feel the friendship deteriorating—not because his friend is angry, but because Tyler is embarrassed, and embarrassment makes people disappear.

He has the money now. His emergency fund is at $400. But taking $300 out would wipe almost all of it. So he keeps putting it off, and the silence gets louder.

Pay it back. Today. Not next week, not "when I have a little more saved." Tyler's emergency fund drops to $100, which stings—but the friendship is worth more than a $300 cushion he can rebuild in thirteen weeks at his current pace. Send the money with a short, honest message: "I'm sorry this took so long. No excuses. Here's the $300." No lengthy explanation. No over-apologizing. Just the money and accountability.

The deeper lesson: informal loans between friends have no structure—no interest rate, no due date, no consequence for not paying. That absence of structure makes them dangerously easy to ignore. Going forward, Tyler doesn't borrow from friends unless he can pay it back within the timeframe he promises. And if he can't commit to that, he says so upfront: "I don't know when I could pay this back." Then the friend can decide whether to gift it or say no—and nobody ends up dodging texts

"I'm drowning and I don't know where to start."

What happened: Jordan has $34,000 in student loans, $1,200 on a credit card from a car repair last year, and just found out she owes $800 in taxes from a freelance project she did on the side. Her monthly student loan payment is $380, the credit card minimum is $36, and the IRS wants its money. She feels paralyzed. Every time she sits down to figure out a plan, the total number ($36,000) makes her want to close the laptop. So she does.

Why it happens: Multiple debts with different interest rates, different servicers, and different urgency levels create decision paralysis. The total feels insurmountable, so the brain's response is avoidance. Jordan isn't lazy or irresponsible. She's overwhelmed by a problem that feels too complex to solve.

What to do: Stop looking at the total. Jordan doesn't owe $36,000 – she owes three separate debts, and each one has its own priority. Step one: handle the IRS. Set up a payment plan at irs.gov (the interest rate is lower than a credit card). Step two: kill the credit card. At $1,200, she can attack this aggressively – $200/month clears it in about seven months. Step three: once the card is gone, redirect that $200 to either extra student loan payments or savings, depending on whether her emergency fund is solid. The student loans aren't going anywhere – they're on a 10-year plan with a manageable rate. She doesn't need to panic about them. She needs to handle the urgent stuff first, then let the system work.

What not to do: Try to attack all three aggressively at the same time. Splitting extra money three ways means none of them gets paid off quickly, and you never get the psychological win of eliminating a debt. Also, don't ignore the IRS – they have more collection power than any other creditor, including the ability to garnish wages without a court order.

Debt is heavy. Not just financially—the weight of owing money follows you into conversations, into sleep, into every purchase decision. If you're carrying it right now, the most important thing in this chapter isn't any specific strategy. It's this: debt is a math problem with a solution, not a moral failing.

Michael didn't get $8,000 in credit card debt because he's irresponsible. Jordan didn't get $34,000 in student loans because she made bad choices. They made normal decisions in a system designed to extend credit to people who can barely afford it. The system worked exactly as intended—just not in their favor.

The way out is the same for everyone: stop the bleeding, pick a method, automate what you can, and let time do the work. You didn't get into debt overnight and you won't get out overnight. But every payment moves the number in the right direction.

Chapter 6: Credit Scores Decoded

> *"Your credit score is like your financial GPA — except it follows you way longer and actually matters." —Tori Dunlap, Her First $100K*

Part 1: What Just Happened to Me?

Jordan stood in the parking lot of the apartment complex, staring at her phone. The property manager had just called. "I'm sorry, but your application was denied. Your credit score is 614."

She'd been so careful. She had a full-time job making $52,000. Two months of pay stubs. A reference from her previous landlord who'd say she always paid on time. She'd saved $4,200 for move-in costs. She thought she was a good candidate—better than good, actually. Responsible. Prepared.

The property manager's voice had been kind but final. "You're welcome to reapply if your score improves."

Jordan sat in her car and Googled "what is a good credit score." The results said 670 was the minimum for "good." She was 56 points short. She didn't even know what that meant. She knew credit scores *existed*—she'd heard people mention them—but she'd never checked hers. She didn't know what went into it. She didn't know that three late payments on a store credit card from sophomore year were still dragging her down two years later, or that her student loan payments—which she'd made on time for a full year—were actually helping but not enough to offset the damage.

She ended up renting from a private landlord who didn't run credit checks. The place was fine, but it was $150 more per month than the apartment she'd wanted. Over a twelve-month lease, her credit score cost her $1,800.

And that was just for an apartment. She didn't even want to think about what it would mean for a car loan.

Jordan felt stupid. Like she'd failed some basic adulting test everyone else had passed. Like this was obvious information and she was the only one who didn't get the memo.

She wasn't stupid. She just didn't know what she didn't know. And the system had punished her for it.

Tyler's Invisibility

Tyler has a different problem: he doesn't exist.

He's never had a credit card. Never taken out a loan. Never financed anything. He's paid cash for everything his entire life. Nobody ever explained how credit worked or why it mattered.

Last month, he tried to get a basic credit card—one of those starter cards advertised to people with "limited credit history." He filled out the application, hit submit, and got an instant denial. The rejection letter arrived a week later: "Insufficient credit history."

He tried a second card. Same result. Two hard inquiries on a credit report that didn't exist, and now he was further behind than when he started.

Tyler isn't a bad risk. He's never missed a payment on anything because he's never owed anyone money. But to the credit system, he's invisible. And invisible is treated the same as risky.

He makes $16,800 a year at the warehouse. He's eighteen. He's trying to do everything right. And the system has locked him out before he even started.

Michael's Shock Discovery

Michael thought his credit was fine. He'd never missed a payment on anything—not his credit cards, not his car loan, not his student loans. He paid his minimums every month like clockwork. That's what you're supposed to do, right?

Then he checked his score for the first time: 582.

He stared at the number. That couldn't be right. He'd been *responsible.* He paid his bills. How was his score worse than Jordan's, who'd actually been late on payments?

He pulled his full credit report and started reading. His utilization was 73%—he owed $8,000 across two cards with a combined limit of $11,000. He didn't know utilization mattered. He thought as long as you paid the minimum, you were fine.

Then he saw the medical collection: $340 from an ER visit two years ago. He'd completely forgotten about it. He'd gone to the ER after a workplace accident, given them his insurance information, and assumed it was handled. He never received a bill—it had gone to his old address. The first time he found out about it was when it showed up on his credit report, already in collections.

Michael felt blindsided. He'd been playing by the rules—or what he thought were the rules—and the game had been scoring him the entire time on criteria he didn't know existed.

The Shame of Not Knowing

All three of them felt the same thing: shame.

Not the shame of having done something wrong, but the shame of not knowing there was something to know. The shame of being punished by a system nobody had explained. The shame of feeling like everyone else got a manual and they didn't.

Jordan felt it when the property manager said her score was too low. Tyler felt it when the second credit card rejection arrived. Michael felt it when he saw 582 and realized he'd been hurting his score for years without knowing it.

That shame is designed into the system. Credit scores are treated like common knowledge—something everyone should just *know*—but nobody teaches them. Not in school. Not in most families. You're expected to figure it out on your own, and if you don't, you pay for it. Literally.

Jordan paid $1,800 in extra rent. Tyler can't get approved for anything. Michael's score is costing him higher interest rates on everything he finances.

The system worked exactly as designed. It just wasn't designed for them.

Part 2: How This Game Actually Works

Jordan spent the weekend after her apartment rejection reading everything she could find about credit scores. She was tired of being punished for not understanding.

What she learned: credit scores aren't a measure of how responsible you are. They're a prediction about your behavior. Specifically, they predict how likely you are to repay borrowed money based on how you've handled credit in the past.

That's it. It's not a judgment of your character. It's not a measure of your intelligence or your worth as a person. It's a risk assessment tool that lenders use to decide whether to give you money and what interest rate to charge.

The most commonly used score is the **FICO score**, which ranges from 300 to 850. There's also **VantageScore**, which uses the same range but calculates differently. Most lenders use FICO, so that's the one that matters most.

What the Numbers Actually Mean

Jordan's 614 put her in the "fair" range. Not terrible, but not good enough for competitive rates or easy approvals.

Credit Score Ranges

Range	Rating	What It Means in Practice
800–850	Exceptional	Best rates on everything. You're a lender's dream.
740–799	Very Good	Excellent rates. Most approvals are easy.
670–739	Good	Decent rates. Most applications approved.
580–669	Fair	Higher rates. Some denials. Limited options.

Range	Rating	What It Means in Practice
300–579	Poor	Frequent denials. Very high rates when approved.

But the real shock came when Jordan looked up what these ranges actually *cost*. She found a calculator that showed interest rates on a $25,000 car loan over 5 years:

Credit Score	Estimated APR	Monthly Payment	Total Interest Paid
750+ (Excellent)	5.0%	$472	$3,307
680 (Good)	7.5%	$501	$5,068
620 (Fair)	12.0%	$556	$8,382
550 (Poor)	18.0%	$635	$13,069

Same car. Same loan amount. Almost $10,000 more in interest between excellent and poor credit.

Jordan stared at the numbers. Her credit score wasn't just costing her $150/month in extra rent. It was a price tag on every loan she'd ever take. Every apartment. Every car. Eventually, a house.

She wasn't angry anymore. She was determined.

The Five Factors (And What Actually Matters)

Michael pulled up his credit report and started cross-referencing it with everything he'd learned. His score was built from five factors, each weighted differently:

FICO Score Breakdown

Factor	Weight	What It Measures	Your Control Level
Payment History	35%	Do you pay on time?	High — just pay on time
Credit Utilization	30%	How much of your available credit are you using?	High — keep balances low
Length of Credit History	15%	How long have you had credit?	Low — just takes time

Factor	Weight	What It Measures	Your Control Level
Credit Mix	10%	Do you have different types of credit?	Medium — don't force it
New Credit Inquiries	10%	Have you applied for a lot of credit recently?	High — apply sparingly

Payment History (35%) was the big one. Every on-time payment helped. Every late payment hurt—and a single 30-day late payment could drop your score 50–100 points.

This was what was killing Jordan. Three late payments on that store card from sophomore year. She'd been nineteen, working part-time, and the due date kept slipping her mind. She'd eventually paid it off, but the damage was done. Those three late marks were still sitting on her report, dragging her score down two years later.

Michael, on the other hand, had perfect payment history. He'd never missed a due date. That 35% was working in his favor.

Credit Utilization (30%) was Michael's problem. He owed $8,000 on $11,000 in total credit limits—73% utilization. He didn't know this mattered. He thought as long as you paid the minimum, you were fine.

He wasn't. Utilization is how much of your available credit you're using, and high utilization tanks your score. The system sees it as a sign you're overextended—that you're relying on credit to get by.

General targets: under 30% is acceptable. Under 10% is ideal. Zero utilization—never using your cards—can actually be slightly worse than low utilization, because lenders want to see you can use credit responsibly, not that you avoid it entirely.

Michael's 73% was screaming "financial stress" to every algorithm that looked at his report.

But here's what gave him hope: utilization has no memory. The moment his balance dropped, his score would reflect it. If he paid down his cards from $8,000 to $3,000, his utilization would drop to 27%, and his score could jump 50+ points within a single statement cycle.

Important detail Jordan learned: Utilization is calculated based on your balance when your statement closes, not after you pay. So even if you pay in full every month (which she does now), a high balance at statement time can temporarily ding your score. If you're about to apply for a loan or apartment, pay down your cards a few days *before* your statement closes.

And a reminder from Chapter 5: to avoid paying interest, you need to pay your *statement balance* (the amount from your previous billing cycle) by the due date—not your current balance, which includes new charges. Pay the statement balance in full and you owe zero interest, even if your current balance shows new purchases.

Length of Credit History (15%) rewards you for having accounts open a long time. This is why you don't close old credit cards, even if you rarely use them. That card you opened at nineteen and forgot about? It's helping your score just by existing.

Jordan's store card—the one that caused all the problems—was also her oldest account. Closing it would shorten her credit history and hurt her score even more. She hated that card, but she was keeping it open.

Tyler's problem was that he had no credit history at all. Zero accounts. Zero payment history. Zero length. He wasn't a bad risk—he was an unknown. And unknown gets treated like risky.

Credit Mix (10%) means having different types of credit—a credit card (revolving), a student loan (installment), a car loan (installment). It's a small factor, and you shouldn't take on debt just to improve your mix. But if you already have different types and pay them on time, it helps.

New Credit Inquiries (10%) — every time you apply for credit, a "hard inquiry" hits your report and can drop your score 5–10 points temporarily. Tyler's two credit card applications had dinged him twice for no benefit.

But here's the exception: when rate-shopping for a mortgage or auto loan, multiple inquiries within a 14–45 day window count as a single inquiry. The system knows you're shopping around, not desperately applying for everything.

Tyler's Plan: Building Credit From Zero

Tyler sat down with his mom and explained what he'd learned. He wasn't asking for money—he was asking for strategy.

His mom had good credit. She'd had the same Visa card for eight years, always paid on time, kept her balance low. Tyler asked if she'd add him as an authorized user. She didn't have to give him the physical card. He'd never spend a dollar on it. But her account history would appear on his credit report, giving him instant credit age.

She agreed.

Then Tyler researched secured credit cards. These are starter cards designed for people with no credit or bad credit. You put down a deposit—say, $200—and that becomes your credit limit. It's your own money, so there's no risk to the lender. You use the card, pay it off, and build a payment history.

Tyler applied for the Discover it® Secured card. $200 deposit, $200 limit. Approved instantly.

His plan:

- **Month 1:** Use the card for gas—one purchase a month, about $40. Pay it off in full before the due date. That's it. Small, consistent, on-time.
- **Month 1 (same day):** Get added as an authorized user on his mom's card. Her eight-year history appears on his report immediately.
- **Month 3:** Sign up for Experian Boost, which adds his phone bill and utility payments to his Experian credit file. Free, takes five minutes.

- **Month 6:** Check his FICO score through Discover (free for cardholders). See where he stands.
- **Month 12:** After a year of on-time payments, Discover will likely offer to upgrade him to an unsecured card and return his deposit.

Tyler wasn't invisible anymore. He was building a credit history—strategically, deliberately, without paying a dime in interest.

Tyler's Credit-Building Timeline

Month	Action	Estimated Score
0	No credit history	N/A (credit invisible)
1	Secured card + authorized user + Experian Boost	580–620
6	6 months on-time payments	640–670
12	Upgrade to unsecured card	680–710
24	2 years of clean history	710–740

Jordan's Plan: Fixing the Damage

Jordan's 614 came from two problems: those three late payments from 2024, and high utilization on her store card.

The late payments were going to take time. They'd stay on her report for seven years, but their impact would fade steadily. At the two-year mark, they'd matter much less than they did at six months. She couldn't erase them. She could only outlast them.

But the utilization? That she could fix immediately.

She owed $400 on a $500 limit—80% utilization on that card. Bringing it under $50 would drop utilization to 10% and could boost her score within one statement cycle.

She also learned she could request a credit limit increase on any card that offered a soft pull (no hard inquiry). Capital One, American Express, and Discover typically do soft pulls for existing customers. Same balance, higher limit, lower utilization ratio.

The script: Call your card issuer or use their online request. Start with: *"I'd like to request a credit limit increase. Before we proceed, can you tell me if this will require a hard inquiry or a soft pull?"* If it's a hard pull, decide if the utilization benefit is worth the small, temporary score impact. If it's a soft pull, go ahead.

Jordan's action plan:

- **Week 1:** Pay down the store card to under $50. Use money from her "life stuff" sinking fund.
- **Week 2:** Request a credit limit increase on her main card (Capital One). If approved, her total available credit goes up, utilization goes down.
- **Week 3:** Pull her full credit reports from all three bureaus at AnnualCreditReport.com. Check for errors. One in five reports contains mistakes—wrong balances, accounts that aren't hers, incorrect late payments. Dispute anything that's wrong.
- **Month 2 onward:** Build a streak of on-time payments. Set every account to autopay. Never miss a due date again.
- **Month 6:** Check her score. See the progress.

She wasn't trying to get to 800. She just needed to get above 670—the threshold for "good" credit. That would qualify her for the apartment she wanted next lease cycle and get her competitive interest rates on a car loan.

Jordan's Score Recovery Projection

Timeline	Actions	Projected Score
Now	614 — three late payments, high utilization	614
2 months	Pay down store card, get limit increase	650–670
6 months	6 months clean payments	680–700
12 months	Full year clean, utilization stays low	700–720
24 months	Late payments aging out of significance	720–740

Jordan printed this table and taped it to her bathroom mirror. Every month, she'd check off another milestone. The number would move. She just had to be patient.

Michael's Realization: It's Not Too Late

Michael's 582 felt like a disaster when he first saw it. But once he understood *why* it was 582, he realized it wasn't permanent damage. It was a snapshot of his current situation—and his situation was fixable.

His payment history was perfect. That 35% was solid. His credit age was decent—he'd had his oldest card for four years. His credit mix was good—two credit cards, a car loan, student loans.

The problem was utilization (73%) and that medical collection ($340).

The collection was sitting there like a landmine. He called the hospital's billing department, explained he'd never received a bill, and asked if they'd recall it from collections if he paid in full. They said no—once it's sold to collections, the hospital can't take it back.

So Michael called the collection agency. He didn't admit the debt was his. He didn't agree to pay. He asked for validation—proof that the debt was legitimate and that they had the right to collect it.

They sent documentation. It was valid. He owed it.

Michael negotiated. "I'll pay this in full today if you agree to remove it from my credit report." The collector said they'd mark it "paid in full" but couldn't remove it.

Michael pushed. "I'm not asking you to lie. I'm asking you to delete it as part of a settlement. I'll pay $340 right now, and you remove the tradeline. Otherwise, I'll set up a payment plan and you'll get $50/month for seven months."

The collector agreed. Michael got it in writing—a pay-for-delete agreement—before he sent the payment. Two weeks later, the collection disappeared from his report.

Then he focused on utilization. He was already paying down his credit card debt through the avalanche method from Chapter 5. As his balance dropped from $8,000 to $6,000 to $4,000, his utilization would fall from 73% to 55% to 36%. His score would climb with every payment.

Michael checked his score three months later: 628. Still not great, but 46 points higher. Six months after that: 670. He'd crossed into "good" territory.

He wasn't done—he wanted to get above 700—but he'd gone from feeling hopeless to understanding exactly what he needed to do.

Part 3: Now I Can Actually Play

The Psychological Shift

Jordan's first reaction to the apartment rejection had been shame. She'd felt stupid, behind, like she'd failed some basic test.

Three months into her recovery plan, she felt something different: control.

She knew what her score was. She knew why it was that number. She knew what actions would move it up and how long it would take. The system wasn't punishing her anymore—she was playing the game strategically.

Her score hit 658 after two months. Not high enough for the apartment she'd wanted, but high enough that she stopped feeling powerless. She was making progress. The number was moving in the right direction.

Tyler felt the same shift. He'd gone from "I'm invisible and locked out" to "I'm building a credit history on purpose." His secured card sat in his wallet. He used it once a month for gas, paid it off immediately, and watched his score appear for the first time: 612. Not great, but it existed. He existed.

Michael's shift was different. He'd thought he was doing everything right, and discovering his 582 had felt like betrayal. But once he understood utilization, once he saw the medical collection disappear, once he watched his score climb from 582 to 628 to 670, he realized something: credit scores aren't a judgment. They're a game. And he'd been playing without knowing the rules.

Now he knew the rules.

Credit Score Myths — Busted

As Jordan, Tyler, and Michael learned the system, they also learned what *wasn't* true—myths that had confused them or cost them money.

"Carrying a balance helps your score." No. This is the most expensive myth in personal finance. You do NOT need to carry a balance and pay interest to build credit. Use your card, pay the statement balance in full before the due date, build credit, pay zero interest. Jordan had believed this myth for years and had paid hundreds in unnecessary interest because of it.

"Checking my own credit hurts my score." No. Checking your own credit is a "soft inquiry" with zero effect on your score. Check monthly if you want. Tyler had been afraid to check his score because he thought it would make things worse. It doesn't.

"Closing cards I don't use is smart." Usually no. Closing cards reduces your total available credit (hurts utilization) and can shorten your credit history. Keep old cards open—use them once a year to keep them active. Exception: if a card has an annual fee you're not getting value from, closing it may make sense. Jordan kept her store card open even though she hated it, because closing it would hurt more than keeping it.

"My income affects my credit score." No. Income doesn't appear on your credit report. A person making $30,000 can have a better score than someone making $300,000. Tyler had assumed his low income was part of why he couldn't get approved. It wasn't. It was the lack of credit history.

"Debit cards build credit." No. Debit cards don't report to credit bureaus. Using one does nothing for your credit score.

Checking Your Credit (And Why It Matters)

Emma had always been cautious about her personal information. When her health insurance company sent a data breach notification, she didn't panic—she acted.

She pulled her credit reports from all three bureaus at AnnualCreditReport.com. That's the only official source for free reports. She checked one bureau every four months to monitor throughout the year.

Everything looked clean. No accounts she didn't recognize. No incorrect late payments. No unauthorized inquiries.

Then she froze her credit at all three bureaus—Equifax, Experian, and TransUnion. A credit freeze prevents anyone (including you) from opening new credit in your name. It's free to freeze and unfreeze.

Emma created PINs for each bureau, saved them in her password manager, and left her credit frozen. When she applied for a new credit card six months later, she temporarily unfroze Experian (the bureau the card issuer used), got approved, and refroze it the same day.

Zero risk. Zero hassle. And if someone tried to open an account in her name, they'd hit a wall.

How to Freeze Your Credit

Bureau	Website
Equifax	equifax.com/personal/credit-report-services/credit-freeze
Experian	experian.com/freeze

Bureau	Website
TransUnion	transunion.com/credit-freeze

Each bureau gives you a PIN to lift the freeze temporarily when you need to apply for credit. It takes about fifteen minutes total to freeze all three. Emma did it on a Saturday morning and hasn't thought about it since—except to feel relieved that her credit is locked down.

Where to Check Your Credit Score (For Free)

Credit reports and credit scores are different. Your report shows your full credit history. Your score is the three-digit number calculated from that history.

Many sources offer free scores:

- Your bank or credit card app (check if it's FICO or VantageScore)
- Credit Karma (VantageScore, not FICO—can differ by 20–50 points)
- Discover's free scorecard (actual FICO, even for non-customers)
- Experian (free FICO)

Important: Credit Karma shows VantageScore, which can differ from FICO by 20–50 points. Most lenders use FICO. If you're about to apply for something important, check a FICO source.

What to Look For on Your Report

Jordan pulled her reports and found two errors: a duplicate entry for her student loan (making it look like she owed twice as much), and an incorrect late payment on a utility bill she'd never been late on.

She disputed both online. The bureaus have 30 days to investigate. For disputes that don't resolve online, send a letter via certified mail:

[Your Name, Address, Date]

Re: Dispute of Inaccurate Information

I am writing to dispute the following item on my credit report: [Account Name, last 4 digits of account number]. This item is inaccurate because [specific reason—e.g., "this account shows a late payment on March 2024, but my records confirm payment was made on time"]. I have enclosed copies of [supporting documents]. Please investigate and correct this error within 30 days as required by the Fair Credit Reporting Act.

Keep copies of everything. Send certified mail with return receipt. The bureau must respond within 30 days. Both errors were removed within three weeks, and her score jumped 12 points.

Credit Report Verification Checklist

Check	Status
All accounts are mine	☐
Personal info is correct	☐
No incorrect late payments	☐
Account statuses are accurate	☐
Balances and limits are right	☐
No duplicate entries	☐
No unauthorized inquiries	☐

One in five credit reports contains an error. Checking yours isn't paranoia—it's maintenance.

Mia's Credit: Thin, Not Bad

Mia's credit situation is different from everyone else's. She has one credit card she pays off monthly and a phone bill in her name. That's it. No student loans, no car payment, no history of late payments—but also not much history at all.

Her score hovers around 650. Not bad, just thin. The system doesn't have enough data to trust her yet. Her variable income makes it harder—some months her utilization spikes when a client pays late and she carries a balance for a cycle, then it drops back down the next month. That volatility dings her score even though she's never actually missed a payment.

Mia's fix is time and consistency. She keeps the card, pays it off, and lets the history build. She's not in crisis. She's just early in the game.

When Bad Credit Matters Less

Tyler's building credit now, but he also realized something: for his current life, a great credit score isn't essential.

He pays cash for everything. He's not buying a house anytime soon. He's not financing a car—he's saving for a used one he can buy outright. His landlord doesn't check credit.

A good credit score gives you options. But if you're not using those options right now, a lower score isn't the crisis it's made out to be.

This isn't permission to ignore your credit—circumstances change, and a good score gives you flexibility you might need later. But if you're stressed about a lower score, consider whether it's actually affecting your life right now or if you're worried about a hypothetical.

Jordan's 614 cost her $1,800 in extra rent. That was real. Tyler's lack of credit history locked him out of credit cards, but he wasn't trying to finance anything, so it didn't hurt him yet. Michael's 582 would've cost him thousands in higher interest rates if he'd needed a car loan, but he already had one.

Context matters. Fix your credit because it gives you options and saves you money. But don't let a number define your worth.

The Game You Can Win

Jordan's sitting in her new apartment now—the one she wanted a year ago. Her score hit 695 last month. The property manager approved her application without hesitation.

Tyler's score is 680. He's had his secured card for eighteen months, got upgraded to an unsecured card, and just applied for a second card to improve his credit mix. Approved.

Michael's at 702. His credit card debt is down to $2,400, his utilization is 22%, and his score has been climbing steadily for a year.

None of them are credit score obsessives. They're not checking their scores daily or optimizing every decision around their FICO number. They just understand the game now.

Pay on time. Keep utilization low. Don't close old accounts. Check your reports for errors. Be patient.

Every month of responsible behavior moves the number in the right direction. And once you understand that it's a game with rules—not a judgment of your character—the shame disappears.

You're not behind. You're learning. And now that you know the rules, you can play.

Your Move

- **Today:** Check your credit score for free at Discover's scorecard or your bank's app. Just look at the number.
- **This week:** Pull your full credit report at AnnualCreditReport.com. Check for errors and accounts you don't recognize.
- **This month:** Freeze your credit at all three bureaus. Fifteen minutes total. Zero cost. Maximum protection.

When It Goes Sideways

"I found out my score is terrible and I don't know why."

What happened: Michael checked his credit score for the first time and saw 582. He knew about the credit card debt, but he expected it to be higher—he'd never missed a payment. Then he pulled his full credit report and discovered two things: his utilization was 73% (which he understood once he learned how utilization works), and there was a $340 medical collection from an ER visit two years ago that he'd completely forgotten about. He never received a bill—it went to an old address.

Why it feels so bad: Michael thought he was doing everything right. He paid his bills on time. He was responsible. Finding out his score was in the "poor" range felt like being punished for something he didn't know he'd done wrong. The medical collection especially felt unfair—he'd gone to the ER, given them his insurance, and assumed it was handled. He didn't know the bill had gone to collections until it showed up on his credit report.

Why it happens: Medical billing is notoriously unreliable. Bills go to wrong addresses, get lost between insurance and provider, or sit in administrative limbo until they're sent to collections without the patient ever knowing. And most people never check their credit reports, so the first time they see these collections is when they get denied for something or finally check their score.

What to do: First, dispute the collection if you don't recognize it or never received proper notice—the collector must prove the debt is valid and that they have the right to collect it. For medical collections under $500, check whether it even appears on your report (as of 2023, medical debt under $500 is excluded from credit reports). If it's valid and over $500, negotiate a pay-for-delete: offer to pay in full in exchange for the collector removing it from your report. Get the agreement in writing before you pay. Michael negotiated his $340 collection down to a pay-for-delete, got it in writing, paid it, and watched it disappear from his report two weeks later.

Then focus on the utilization. As Michael pays down his credit card debt through the avalanche method from Chapter 5, his score will climb. He could see a 50–80 point improvement from utilization alone within a few months. Three months after removing the collection and paying down his cards, his score jumped from 582 to 628. Six months later, it hit 670.

What not to do: Don't ignore it and hope it goes away. Collections sit on your report for 7 years. Don't pay the collection without negotiating removal first—paying it changes the status to "paid collection" but it still sits on your report, and "paid collection" only helps marginally with newer scoring models. And don't assume your score is permanently damaged. Michael went from 582 to 702 in fourteen months. It's fixable.

"I have no credit and I can't get approved for anything."

What happened: Tyler applied for a basic credit card to start building credit and got denied. The rejection letter said "insufficient credit history." He tried a second card—denied again. Two hard inquiries, zero cards, and now he's further behind than when he started. He felt locked out of a system he was trying to enter responsibly.

Why it feels so bad: Tyler wasn't trying to do anything risky. He wasn't applying for a $10,000 limit or a rewards card with perks. He was applying for a starter card designed for people with limited history. Getting denied twice felt like the system was telling him he didn't belong. And the hard inquiries from the denials made his (nonexistent) credit situation worse.

Why it happens: It's the classic credit catch-22. You need credit to build credit, but nobody will give you credit without a history. The system is designed for people who already have credit, and it leaves newcomers—especially young adults, immigrants, and anyone who's always paid cash—locked out. Tyler wasn't a bad risk. He was an unknown. And unknown gets treated the same as risky.

What to do: Stop applying for regular credit cards. Each denial adds a hard inquiry that makes the next application harder. Instead, follow Tyler's path: get a secured card (which requires a deposit, not a credit history), become an authorized user on a family member's account (their history appears on your report), and use Experian Boost to get credit for bills you're already paying (phone, utilities). Within six months, you'll have enough history to qualify for a starter unsecured card.

Tyler got a Discover it® Secured card with a $200 deposit. His mom added him as an authorized user on her eight-year-old Visa (he never got the physical card or spent a dollar on it). He signed up for Experian Boost and added his phone bill. Six months later, his score was 655 and he got approved for his first unsecured card. Two denials aren't permanent damage—hard inquiries only affect your score for about a year and fall off after two.

What not to do: Don't apply for more cards hoping one will say yes. Each application is a hard inquiry. Don't accept a predatory "credit building" card with a $300 limit and $200 in annual fees—those exist and they target exactly this situation. And don't pay a "credit repair" company to fix something that isn't broken. You don't have bad credit. You have no credit. The solution is building it, not repairing it.

"Someone opened accounts in my name."

What happened: Emma pulled her annual credit report and found a Capital One card she didn't open with a $2,300 balance—and three months of missed payments. Her score had dropped 85 points. She'd never applied for a Capital One card. Someone had used her personal information to open a fraudulent account.

Why it feels so bad: Emma had been careful. She didn't click suspicious links. She used strong passwords. She monitored her accounts. And still, someone stole her identity and trashed her credit. The missed payments weren't hers, but they were destroying her score. She felt violated and powerless—like the system was punishing her for someone else's crime.

Why it happens: Data breaches are constant. Your Social Security number, address, and date of birth have probably been compromised in at least one breach. Criminals use this information to open accounts, run up charges, and disappear. Federal employees like Emma—whose personal data was exposed in the massive OPM breach—are especially vulnerable. It's not about what you did wrong. It's about living in a world where your information has been stolen and sold dozens of times.

What to do: Act fast. Place a fraud alert with one bureau (they're required to notify the other two)—this makes it harder for someone to open new accounts. Then freeze your credit at all three bureaus to prevent additional fraudulent accounts. File a report at IdentityTheft.gov—this creates an official FTC Identity Theft Report you'll need for disputes. Dispute the fraudulent account with all three bureaus, including your FTC report as documentation. File a police report for additional documentation. Contact Capital One's fraud department directly to report the account as unauthorized.

Emma did all of this within 48 hours of discovering the fraud. The fraudulent account, missed payments, and hard inquiry were all removed once the investigation confirmed fraud. Her score recovered within two months. She also froze her credit at all three bureaus and now keeps it permanently frozen, unfreezing temporarily only when she needs to apply for something.

What not to do: Don't pay anything on the fraudulent account. Making a payment could be interpreted as accepting the debt. Don't just dispute online and assume it's handled—follow up with certified mail and keep copies of everything. Don't ignore it because you're overwhelmed—identity theft gets worse if you don't act quickly. And if you haven't already, freeze your credit at all three bureaus after resolving this. Emma's credit has been frozen for two years now. It takes five minutes to unfreeze when she needs to, and the rest of the time, she's protected.

Your credit score isn't a judgment of your character. It's a game with rules—and now you know them.

Every month of responsible behavior moves the number in the right direction.

Chapter 7: Investing Isn't Just for Rich People

> *"You don't need to be an expert. You just need to start." — JL Collins, The Simple Path to Wealth*

Emma started contributing to her TSP on day one of her federal job. She didn't understand investing — she just picked the lifecycle fund her HR orientation recommended, set her contribution to 5% to get the full agency match, and forgot about it.

Fourteen months later, she logged into TSP.gov for the first time since enrollment. She expected to see roughly what she'd put in — maybe $4,700 in contributions. Instead, the balance was $6,200. The agency match had added another $3,400, and market growth had added $100 on top. She'd made $3,500 in free money and growth while doing absolutely nothing.

Tyler, meanwhile, has invested exactly $0. He doesn't have a 401(k) — the warehouse doesn't offer one. He doesn't have an IRA because he doesn't know what an IRA is. He's eighteen, making $16,800 a year, and the idea of investing feels like something for people in a completely different financial universe.

It's not. And the gap between Tyler and Emma is going to grow exponentially every year he waits.

Here's a lie you might believe: investing is for people with money. Real money. Suit-wearing, German-car-driving, "I'll have my advisor look into it" money.

It's not. Investing is for you. And the biggest advantage you have right now — the one thing that beats having a lot of money — is time.

Why Investing Matters More Than Saving

Inflation Is Eating Your Savings

Inflation means prices go up over time. Average inflation runs about 2–3% per year historically. If your money sits in a regular savings account earning 0.01%, you're losing purchasing power every year. $10,000 in a savings account today will still say $10,000 in ten years, but it'll only buy what roughly $7,500 buys today.

Your HYSA from Chapter 4 helps — 3–4% keeps pace with inflation. But it doesn't grow your wealth. Investing does.

Time Beats Amount

Here's what happens when two people invest $200/month at a 7% average annual return, but start at different ages:

The Cost of Waiting: $200/Month at 7% Average Return

Investor	Starts At	Invests Until 65	Total Contributed	Balance at 65
Tyler	Age 18	47 years	$112,800	$877,000
Jordan	Age 23	42 years	$100,800	$609,000
Emma	Age 24	41 years	$98,400	$565,000
Michael	Age 26	39 years	$93,600	$487,000
Someone	Age 35	30 years	$72,000	$244,000

Tyler invests $40,800 more than the person who starts at 35. But he ends up with $633,000 more. That's compound growth — your money earns returns, those returns earn returns, and the snowball effect accelerates over decades. Every year you wait costs more than the year before.

Investing Basics: What Are You Actually Buying?

Stocks — You're buying a tiny piece of ownership in a company. If it does well, your piece becomes worth more. Individual stocks are risky. Even great companies can crash.

Bonds — You're lending money to a company or government. They pay you interest, then return your principal. Safer than stocks, lower returns. The stable part of a portfolio.

Mutual Funds — Pool money from many investors to buy a collection of stocks, bonds, or both. Professional managers choose what to buy and sell. This costs money — mutual funds charge expense ratios (fees) that eat into your returns.

Index Funds and ETFs — This is where it gets good for regular people.

An index fund doesn't try to pick winners. It buys everything in a particular index — like the S&P 500 (the 500 largest U.S. companies). Instead of paying someone to pick stocks (and usually get it wrong), you're buying the whole market at once for almost nothing in fees.

ETFs (Exchange-Traded Funds) work similarly but trade like stocks throughout the day. Many ETFs are index funds.

Why Index Funds Win

Factor	Index Fund	Actively Managed Fund
Expense ratio (annual fee)	0.03–0.20%	0.50–1.50%+
Beat the market long-term?	Matches it (which beats most managers)	Over 90% underperform over 15–20 years
Diversification	Hundreds or thousands of companies	Manager's picks
Effort required from you	Zero	Zero (but you're paying someone to guess)

Over 90% of actively managed funds underperform their benchmark indexes over 15–20 year periods, according to S&P Global's SPIVA research. The boring strategy wins.

Specific Funds to Look For

These are examples, not recommendations. Do your own research and invest based on your situation and risk tolerance. Expense ratios are subject to change — verify current rates before investing.

Index	Fidelity	Vanguard	Schwab
S&P 500	FXAIX (0.015%)	VOO / VFIAX (0.03%)	SWPPX (0.02%)
Total U.S. Market	FSKAX (0.015%)	VTI / VTSAX (0.03%)	SWTSX (0.03%)
Total International	FTIHX (0.06%)	VXUS / VTIAX (0.08%)	—

For most beginners, a Total U.S. Stock Market or S&P 500 index fund is the way to go. One fund. Done.

Where to Put Your Money: Account Types

The account type matters — a lot — because of taxes.

401(k) / TSP

A **401(k)** is a retirement account through your private-sector employer. The **Thrift Savings Plan (TSP)** is the federal government's equivalent for federal employees and military members. Same concept, different system.

The employer/agency match is free money. Many employers match a percentage of what you contribute. Common structures: "100% match up to 3%" means if you contribute 3%, they add another 3% — an instant 100% return. For TSP, the federal government automatically contributes 1% of your salary and matches up to 4% more, for a total of 5% if you contribute at least 5%.

If your employer offers a match and you're not contributing enough to get the full match, you are leaving free money on the table. This should be priority #1 after a basic emergency fund.

2026 contribution limits: $24,500/year (or $32,500 if you're 50+, and $35,750 if you're 60–63)

Traditional vs. Roth: The Tax Decision

Both 401(k) and TSP offer Traditional and Roth options. This decision matters.

Traditional — Contributions come out before taxes. You pay less tax now. You pay income tax on everything you withdraw in retirement.

Roth — Contributions come out after taxes. No tax break now. All growth and withdrawals are completely tax-free in retirement.

The Seed vs. The Harvest

Would you rather pay taxes on the seed or the harvest?

	Traditional	Roth
Tax break	Now (reduces current taxable income)	Later (tax-free withdrawals in retirement)
Contribute $400/month for 40 years	$192,000 total contributions	$192,000 total contributions
At 7% return, grows to	$1,050,000	$1,050,000
Tax bill	Owe taxes on $1,050,000 as you withdraw	$0 — it's all yours

With Traditional, you avoided taxes on $192,000 over the years but owe taxes on $1,050,000 in retirement. With Roth, you paid taxes on $192,000 as you contributed and the $1,050,000 is yours — every penny.

For most people reading this book, Roth is the better choice. You're likely in one of the lowest tax brackets you'll ever be in. Pay taxes now while they're cheap and let decades of growth happen tax-free.

One catch: Even if you contribute to a Roth 401(k) or Roth TSP, any employer/agency match goes into the Traditional (pre-tax) side. That's just how the rules work. You'll end up with both types regardless — which actually gives you flexibility in retirement.

Emma's TSP: A Closer Look

Emma is contributing 5% of her $68,000 salary to Traditional TSP. Her agency matches 5% total (1% automatic + 4% match). That's $6,800/year going in — $3,400 from her, $3,400 from the government.

But here's what she should reconsider: at 24 and $68,000, she's in the 22% federal bracket. She'll almost certainly be in a higher bracket by her forties. Switching her contributions to **Roth TSP** means paying 22% tax on that $3,400 now instead of paying a higher rate on a much larger sum in retirement. The agency match still goes to Traditional TSP no matter what — but her own contributions should be Roth.

TSP Fund Options

The TSP offers a simpler menu than most 401(k) plans:

Fund	What It Invests In	Risk Level
C Fund	S&P 500 (large U.S. companies)	Higher
S Fund	Small/mid U.S. companies	Higher
I Fund	International companies	Higher
F Fund	U.S. bonds	Lower
G Fund	Government securities	Lowest
L Funds	Lifecycle (auto-adjusts over time)	Varies by target date

Emma is currently in the L 2065 Fund — a lifecycle fund that automatically shifts from aggressive to conservative as she approaches retirement. It's a solid set-it-and-forget-it option. If she wanted more growth and is comfortable with volatility, she could allocate more to the C and S Funds directly. But the L Fund is a perfectly reasonable choice, especially at 24 with 41 years until retirement.

IRA (Individual Retirement Account)

An IRA is a retirement account you open yourself, separate from your employer. Essential for people whose jobs don't offer a 401(k) — like Tyler.

2026 contribution limits: $7,500/year (or $8,600 if you're 50+)

Roth IRA is usually the better choice for young earners. Contributions are after-tax, all growth and withdrawals are tax-free, and you can withdraw your *contributions* (not earnings) anytime without penalty. That last point makes it the most flexible retirement account.

Roth IRA income limits: Full contribution up to $150,000 (single) or $236,000 (married filing jointly). If you eventually earn above these limits, there's a strategy called the "backdoor Roth IRA" that gets around it — that's a topic for the Intelligent Wealth series.

HSA (Health Savings Account)

If you have a high-deductible health plan (HDHP), you may have access to the most tax-advantaged account that exists:

Contributions are tax-deductible. Growth is tax-free. Withdrawals for medical expenses are tax-free. Triple tax advantage. Nothing else does this.

2026 contribution limits: $4,400 (individual) or $8,750 (family)

The power move: Contribute to your HSA, invest it (don't just leave it as cash), pay current medical expenses out of pocket if you can, and let the HSA grow for decades.

The Account Priority Order

With multiple account types available, here's where your money should go first:

Investment Priority Order

Priority	Account	Why
1	401(k) / TSP up to employer match	Free money — instant 50–100% return
2	Pay off high-interest debt	No investment reliably beats 20%+ credit card rates
3	Roth IRA (max $7,500)	More investment choices, lower fees than most 401(k)s, flexible withdrawals
4	HSA (if available)	Triple tax advantage is unbeatable
5	401(k) / TSP beyond the match	Up to $24,500 annual limit
6	Taxable brokerage account	No tax advantages, but no restrictions either

Vesting: When the Match Is Actually Yours

Your own contributions are always 100% yours. The employer match? That often comes with strings attached.

Vesting is the process by which employer contributions become yours to keep. Common schedules: immediate vesting (you own the match from day one), cliff vesting (0% until you hit a milestone — usually 3 years — then 100%), or graded vesting (gradually increasing over 3–6 years).

Emma's TSP contributions are immediately vested — that's standard for federal employees. Jordan's 401(k) uses three-year cliff vesting. If she leaves before hitting three years, she loses the match. Worth knowing before accepting a new job offer.

What Happens When You Leave a Job

Your options: leave the 401(k) where it is, roll it into your new employer's plan, roll it into an IRA (often the best choice — more investment options, lower fees), or cash it out (almost always a bad idea — you'll owe income taxes plus a 10% penalty if you're under 59½).

If you roll over, request a **direct rollover** — the money goes straight from one account to the other. If they send you a check, they'll withhold 20% for taxes and you'll have 60 days to deposit the full amount or face penalties.

How to Actually Start

Tyler's Path: No 401(k), No Problem

Tyler's warehouse job doesn't offer a retirement plan. But he can still invest.

Step 1: Open a Roth IRA at Fidelity, Vanguard, or Schwab. Free. Takes 15 minutes online. He needs his Social Security number and a bank account to link.

Step 2: Set up automatic contributions of $25/week ($100/month). This comes out of his checking every Friday, same day as his emergency fund transfer.

Step 3: Buy one fund. Tyler picks a Total U.S. Stock Market index fund (VTI at Vanguard, FSKAX at Fidelity, SWTSX at Schwab). One purchase. Done.

Step 4: Turn on dividend reinvestment (DRIP) — a setting in his account that automatically reinvests any dividends to buy more shares. Set it once, forget it.

Step 5: Don't touch it. Don't check it daily. Let it work.

$100/month at 18 doesn't sound like much. At 7% average return, it's over $438,000 by age 65. If Tyler increases his contributions as his income grows — even just $25 more per month every year or two — that number climbs well past half a million.

Mia's Path: No Employer, No Problem

Mia doesn't have a 401(k) or TSP. Nobody's matching her contributions. She's on her own—and the system wasn't designed for her.

Most investing advice assumes you have an employer handing you a retirement plan with a match. Mia doesn't. She has to build the whole thing herself. The upside: she has more control. The downside: nobody's going to do it for her.

Step 1: Roth IRA (start here). Same as Tyler. She can contribute up to $7,500/year regardless of how she earns her income. She opens one at Fidelity, sets up a $50 transfer on the 1st and 15th of every month ($100/month, $1,200/year), and buys the same total market index fund Tyler uses. On her good months—the $3,500 ones—she throws an extra $200 or $300 in. On lean months, the automatic $100 keeps running.

Step 2: SEP-IRA (when income grows). A SEP-IRA is a retirement account designed for self-employed people. The contribution limit is much higher than a Roth IRA—up to 25% of net self-employment income, maxing out at $70,000 for 2026.

Here's what that looks like at different income levels:

Mia's Net Self-Employment Income	Max SEP-IRA Contribution (25%)
$25,000	$6,250
$35,000	$8,750
$50,000	$12,500
$75,000	$18,750

The SEP-IRA is a Traditional (pre-tax) account—contributions reduce Mia's taxable income now, which also reduces her self-employment tax bill. That's a real advantage for someone already paying the 15.3% SE tax on every dollar.

The order for Mia: Roth IRA first (tax-free growth for decades is too valuable to skip at her age), then SEP-IRA once her income consistently supports higher contributions. She can have both open at the same time.

What Mia doesn't need right now: A solo 401(k), which allows even higher contributions but has more paperwork. That's a tool for when freelancing becomes a serious business with real revenue. The Intelligent Wealth series covers the full self-employed investing and tax strategy playbook.

What to Invest In: Three Options

Option 1: Single index fund. A Total U.S. Stock Market or S&P 500 index fund. One fund, instant diversification, rock-bottom fees. This is what Tyler does. Simple.

Option 2: Two-fund portfolio. U.S. Total Stock Market (80–90%) and International Stock Market (10–20%). Global diversification without the drag of bonds. At your age, you have decades to ride out every market crash — bonds solve a volatility problem you don't have yet. You can add a bond allocation later, typically in your late thirties or forties as retirement gets closer. That transition is covered in the Intelligent Wealth series.

Option 3: Target-date fund. Pick the fund closest to your retirement year (2065 for someone who's 24). It automatically adjusts from aggressive to conservative over time — meaning it's almost entirely stocks right now and gradually adds bonds as you age. One fund, completely hands-off. Slightly higher fees than building your own portfolio, but better than not investing. Emma's L 2065 Fund in the TSP works exactly this way.

What to Expect (Including the Scary Parts)

The market will drop. Not might. Will. It drops 10%+ about once a year. It drops 20%+ every few years. It dropped roughly 34% in early 2020 (COVID crash) and recovered within months.

The COVID Crash: Two Investors, Two Outcomes

	Investor A (Panicked)	Investor B (Did Nothing)
January 2020	$10,000 invested	$10,000 invested
March 23, 2020 (bottom)	Sold everything at $6,600	Held. Kept contributing.
End of 2020	$6,600 in savings account	$11,800
End of 2021	Still in cash, afraid to re-enter	$15,200
End of 2026	$6,600 (missed entire recovery)	$19,500

Same starting point. Same market. One decision made a $13,000 difference. The biggest risk in investing isn't a market crash — it's panic selling during one.

Your job during a downturn: do nothing. Keep contributing if you can. Wait. The investors who build the most wealth are the ones who set up automatic contributions and then don't look at their accounts for years.

Common Beginner Mistakes

Waiting until you have "enough." There's no minimum to start. You can buy fractional shares with $5. Start now, increase later.

Trying to time the market. Professional investors can't do this consistently. You won't be the exception. Time *in* the market beats tim*ing* the market.

Checking too often. Looking at your investments daily is a recipe for anxiety and bad decisions. Check quarterly at most.

Picking individual stocks. Index funds beat most professional stock pickers. Your coworker's "guaranteed" tip isn't a strategy.

Paying high fees. A 1% fee doesn't sound like much, but over 40 years it can cost hundreds of thousands.

The Real Cost of Fees: $200/Month for 40 Years at 7% Gross Return

Expense Ratio	Balance at 65	Lost to Fees
0.03% (index fund)	$521,000	—
0.50%	$457,000	$64,000
1.00%	$398,000	$123,000

That 1% fee costs $123,000 over a career. Read the expense ratio before you buy anything.

Investing isn't complicated. The financial industry wants you to think it is so they can charge you fees to help.

Start as early as you can. Contribute consistently. Buy low-cost index funds. Don't panic when the market drops. Wait a few decades.

You now know more than most people.

Your Move

- **Today:** Check whether your employer offers a retirement plan match. If yes, find out the percentage.
- **This week:** If you have a 401(k) or TSP, log in. Check your contribution rate, your fund choices, and their expense ratios. If you don't have employer access, open a Roth IRA at Fidelity, Vanguard, or Schwab.
- **This month:** Set up automatic contributions. Even $25/week. Buy a total market index fund. Turn on dividend reinvestment. Then close the app.

When It Goes Sideways

"The market dropped 20% and I want to sell everything."

What happened: Michael started investing six months ago — $200/month into a Roth IRA, split between a total market fund and an S&P 500 fund. He'd accumulated about $1,300. Then the market dropped 20% over three weeks. His balance showed $1,040. He watched it fall $50 in a single day. He opened Fidelity on his phone six times that afternoon. He wanted to sell everything and move it to his savings account before it dropped more.

Why it happens: Watching money disappear from your account triggers the same survival instinct as any other threat. Your brain screams "stop the bleeding" — and selling feels like stopping the bleeding. Financial media makes it worse: every headline is about how bad things are, how much further they could fall, how this time might be different. Nobody runs a headline that says "This is normal and everything will probably be fine in two years."

What to do: Close the app. Seriously. Michael's $1,040 is money he doesn't need for 39 years. A 20% drop today is meaningless at age 65. If he keeps contributing $200/month during the downturn, he's buying shares at a 20% discount — those discounted shares will be worth the most when the market recovers. Turn off push notifications from your brokerage app. Set a rule: check your investments once a quarter, max. If you can't resist, delete the app and log in through a browser — the extra steps slow down the impulse.

What not to do: Sell. If you sell at the bottom, you lock in the loss and miss the recovery. Every major drop in market history has been followed by recovery and new highs. Also, don't stop contributing — this is actually when automatic investing helps you the most. It's called **dollar-cost averaging**: by investing the same amount every month regardless of what the market is doing, you buy more shares when prices are low and fewer when prices are high. Michael's $200/month buys roughly 4 shares at $50 each during normal times. During a 20% drop, that same $200 buys 5 shares at $40 each. When the market recovers, those extra shares bought at a discount are worth the most. Staying consistent through a downturn is how regular investors build serious wealth. And don't move retirement money to cash "temporarily" — most people who move to cash after a crash wait too long to get back in and miss the rebound.

"I have no idea what I'm invested in at work."

What happened: Jordan enrolled in her company's 401(k) during her first week, picked a contribution rate of 4% because it sounded reasonable, and selected investments by clicking on whatever had the most impressive-sounding name. She hasn't looked at it since. Eighteen months later, she checks and discovers she's in three actively managed funds with expense ratios between 0.65% and 1.20%, and her portfolio is 45% bonds — extremely conservative for a 23-year-old with 42 years until retirement.

Why it happens: 401(k) enrollment is usually buried in the avalanche of paperwork during your first week at a new job. You're learning names, finding the bathroom, trying not to look lost — and then someone asks you to make decisions about investment allocations. Most people pick something and never revisit it. The fund names are deliberately confusing, and the default options are often conservative (the company doesn't want to get blamed if your aggressive portfolio drops).

What to do: Log into your 401(k) portal today. Look at three things: your contribution rate (are you getting the full match?), your expense ratios (anything over 0.50% for a basic fund is too high), and your allocation (at 23, you should be 80–90%+ in stocks, not 45% bonds). Switch to the lowest-cost index funds available in your plan — most 401(k)s offer at least one S&P 500 or total market index fund. If the only options have high fees, look for the target-date fund closest to your retirement year — these are usually the cheapest option in bad 401(k) plans. Then bump your contribution to at least whatever gets the full employer match.

What not to do: Assume it doesn't matter because "it's just a few percent." Jordan's 1.20% expense ratio fund will cost her over $100,000 more in fees than a 0.03% index fund over her career. Also, don't leave your account at 45% bonds. At 23, that allocation is leaving hundreds of thousands in growth on the table.

"My friend says crypto is better than index funds."

Tyler's coworker won't stop talking about a cryptocurrency that "10x'd" last year. He's showing screenshots of his gains and pressuring Tyler to ditch his "boring" index funds. Tyler starts feeling like his $100/month in VTI is a waste of time.

Ask Tyler's coworker one question: what's your *total* return across *everything* you've bought?

He won't want to answer. Because the screenshots show the win. They don't show the three other coins that lost 60%, the panic-sell during a crash that cost him $800, or the fact that his total return—counting everything—is actually worse than the S&P 500 over the same period. This is survivorship bias in action: people who make money on speculative bets talk about it. People who lose money stay quiet. It creates the illusion that everyone is getting rich except you.

Tyler's move: smile, nod, keep buying VTI. His $100/month in a total market index fund, invested consistently from age 18 to 65, will almost certainly outperform his coworker's crypto portfolio. Not because index funds have the best returns in any given year—they don't. Because Tyler will actually hold for 47 years while his coworker chases the next hot thing, panic-sells, takes profits too early, or rides a coin down 90%.

If Tyler wants crypto exposure, fine—$20/month from discretionary money, separate account, treated as entertainment.

But his Roth IRA is for building wealth over decades, and that means index funds. Boring wins

Investing feels like the most intimidating topic in this book. It's also the one that matters most over time.

Emma's TSP balance grew by $3,500 in fourteen months while she did nothing. Tyler hasn't started yet, but $100/month from age 18 gives him a 47-year runway that no amount of catch-up contributions at 40 can replicate. Jordan's three expensive funds are getting swapped for one cheap index fund, and the fee savings alone will be worth tens of thousands over her career.

You don't need to pick the perfect fund. You don't need to time the market. You don't need to understand options, crypto, or whatever your coworker is hyped about this week. You need to open an account, buy a broad index fund, set up automatic contributions, and leave it alone.

The hardest part is starting. Everything after that is patience.

Chapter 8: Adulting Expenses They Don't Warn You About

"Being an adult is mostly just Googling how to do stuff." — Unknown (but accurate)

Jordan sat on the floor of her empty apartment—her first solo place—and opened her banking app. Rent was paid. Security deposit cleared. First month's utilities set up. She'd been so careful with the budget.

The balance showed $340.

Three weeks ago, she'd had $4,200 saved. She thought she was prepared. She'd calculated rent ($1,100), renters insurance ($18/month), internet ($65). She'd even added a $500 buffer for "miscellaneous."

What she hadn't calculated: the second security deposit the utility company required because she had no credit history with them ($150). The furniture she actually needed to function—not luxury stuff, just a bed frame, a mattress, a desk, a table, two chairs ($1,400, and that was shopping sales). The shower curtain, bath mat, trash cans, dish soap, laundry detergent, toilet paper, paper towels, cleaning supplies, hangers, and the forty other things that cost $8–$25 each but somehow added up to $380 in a single Target trip. Her first electric bill—$95, when she'd assumed utilities were included in rent.

She wasn't irresponsible. She'd researched. She'd budgeted. She'd done everything the internet told her to do.

And she still felt blindsided.

Sitting there on the floor, Jordan felt something she hadn't expected: shame. Like she'd failed some basic adulting test everyone else had passed. Like she should have known better. Like this was obvious and she was the only one who didn't get the memo.

She wasn't. Nobody gets the memo. That's the problem.

Part 1: Your First Independent Year (When Everything Costs More Than You Think)

The first time you're financially independent—whether that's moving out, getting off your parents' phone plan, or losing access to their insurance—you discover a truth nobody prepared you for: adulthood has a cover charge.

It's not just that things cost money. It's that *everything* costs money, including things you didn't know were things.

The Apartment Move-In Shock

Tyler's still living with roommates, splitting a $1,800 three-bedroom. His share is $600, plus about $50 in utilities. It's cramped and the kitchen's a disaster, but it's cheap and he's focused on building his emergency fund.

Jordan wanted her own space. She makes $52,000, and a $1,100 studio felt doable—exactly 25% of her gross income, right in the recommended range. On paper, it worked.

What the "recommended range" doesn't tell you is that the first month isn't one month of rent. It's:

- First month's rent: $1,100
- Security deposit: $1,100 (sometimes refundable, but you're out the cash for now)
- Utility setup fees: $150 (deposits for electric and gas because no credit history with the utility company)
- Renters insurance: $18/month, but they wanted the first six months upfront: $108
- Internet installation: $100 (they waived it if she signed a two-year contract, which she did, which locked her into $65/month even though her building has cheaper options)

Total before she even moved in: $2,558.

Then the furniture. Jordan didn't want much—she's not trying to fill a showroom. But you can't sleep on the floor. You need somewhere to sit. If you work from home even occasionally, you need a desk.

- Bed frame and mattress (IKEA, nothing fancy): $650
- Desk and chair: $280
- Small kitchen table and two chairs: $180
- Lamp, because the overhead light is depressing: $45
- Pots, pans, plates, silverware, glasses: $190
- Bathroom basics (shower curtain, bath mat, towels): $85

Furniture and essentials: $1,430.

Then the stuff you don't think about until you need it: trash cans, a plunger, a broom, a mop, dish soap, laundry detergent, toilet paper, paper towels, cleaning spray, sponges, hangers, a drying rack, a can opener, scissors, a cutting board. None of it expensive individually. All of it adding up to $380 in one trip.

Total move-in cost: $4,368.

Jordan had saved $4,200. She thought she was being responsible. She ended up $168 short and had to put the last of the household stuff on a credit card.

She felt stupid. She wasn't stupid. She just didn't know what she didn't know.

The First Utility Bill

Jordan's lease said "tenant pays utilities." She'd lived in dorms and then in a place where utilities were included, so she'd never actually seen a bill. She Googled "average electric bill" and saw $100–$150. She budgeted $125.

Her first bill was $95. Not bad. She felt relieved.

Her second bill—the first one that covered a full month—was $140. It was July. She'd been running the AC. The third bill, in August, was $168.

She hadn't done anything wrong. She just didn't know that "average" means nothing when you're in a top-floor studio with terrible insulation in a city with a brutal summer. She didn't know that the $100–$150 range assumes a two-person household, not someone living alone who's home all day working remotely.

She adjusted her budget. But the first few months, every bill felt like a surprise attack.

The Stuff That Keeps Coming

Michael's been in his apartment for two years. He's past the move-in shock. But he's learned that the costs don't stop—they just change form.

His building requires renters insurance, so that's $22/month. Internet is $65. Electric averages $110, gas is $35 in winter and $0 in summer. His phone bill—he's finally off his parents' plan—is $70. Subscriptions he actually uses: Spotify ($11), Netflix ($15.50), gym ($45). Household supplies—toilet paper, paper towels, dish soap, laundry detergent, trash bags, cleaning supplies—run about $40/month.

That's $378/month in costs that aren't rent or food. Nearly $4,600/year. None of it feels significant in the moment. All of it disappears from his account every month.

And that's before the irregular stuff: his building's annual pest control fee ($75), the HVAC filter he's supposed to replace every three months ($15 each), the shower curtain liner that got moldy ($12), the light bulbs that burned out ($18 for the pack), the toilet that started running and added $40 to his water bill before he figured out how to fix it.

Adulthood is death by a thousand $15 purchases.

Part 2: The Ongoing Hidden Costs (Insurance, Taxes, and the Car You Thought You Could Afford)

The move-in shock is brutal, but it's one-time. The harder thing is the ongoing costs that nobody explains until you're already committed.

Insurance: Paying for Problems You Don't Have Yet

Tyler's still on his parents' health insurance. He's 23, healthy, hasn't been to a doctor in two years. Insurance feels theoretical.

Then he had a workplace accident. A box fell off a high shelf and hit his shoulder. His manager sent him to the ER. X-rays, an exam, a sling, thirty minutes of a doctor's time.

Three weeks later, a bill arrived for $4,200.

His insurance paid $1,800. He owed $2,400—his deductible plus coinsurance. He had $500 in his emergency fund.

Tyler didn't understand. He *had* insurance. Wasn't that supposed to cover this?

It did cover it—sort of. His parents' plan is a high-deductible health plan (HDHP). Lower monthly premiums, higher out-of-pocket costs. He's responsible for the first $2,000 (the deductible), and then insurance pays 80% and he pays 20% (coinsurance) until he hits the out-of-pocket maximum ($6,000).

Nobody had explained this to him. He'd never needed to know.

Now he knows.

How health insurance actually works:

You pay a **premium** every month just to have coverage. That's the membership fee. Then, when you actually use it:

1. You pay the **deductible**—the amount you're responsible for before insurance kicks in. (Tyler's: $2,000/year)
2. After that, you pay **coinsurance**—your share of the cost, usually 10–20%. (Tyler's: 20%)

3. Once you hit the **out-of-pocket maximum**, insurance covers 100%. (Tyler's: $6,000/year)

For a healthy 23-year-old, a high-deductible plan makes sense—lower premiums, and you're betting you won't need much care. But when something happens, the bill is real.

Tyler called the hospital's billing department. He was terrified they'd say "pay it all now or we're sending you to collections." Instead, they offered him a payment plan—$160/month for 12 months, no interest. He took it. His emergency fund stayed intact.

He also started researching what happens when he turns 26 and loses access to his parents' plan. He has three years to prepare, but now he knows it's coming.

Renters Insurance: The $18/Month You Skip Until You Need It

Jordan didn't get renters insurance for her first two months. It felt like an unnecessary expense—$18/month for something that probably wouldn't happen.

Then her upstairs neighbor's washing machine flooded. Water came through the ceiling, soaked her closet, and fried her laptop.

Without insurance, she would've eaten $1,800 in losses. With the policy she finally signed up for after the fact (too late for this claim), future incidents would be covered.

Renters insurance is cheap because the risk is low. But when the risk happens, it's devastating. It covers your stuff (theft, fire, water damage), liability (if someone gets hurt in your apartment), and additional living expenses (if your place becomes uninhabitable and you need a hotel).

Jordan signed up the day after the flood. She wished she'd done it two months earlier.

The Car That Costs Twice What You Thought

Michael's car payment is $385/month. When he bought it, that felt manageable. He makes $55,000. A $385 payment is less than 10% of his gross income. Totally reasonable.

What he didn't budget for:

- **Insurance:** $190/month ($2,280/year). It jumped $40/month when he moved to a new zip code.
- **Gas:** $160/month for his 25-mile commute.
- **Maintenance:** Oil changes every 5,000 miles ($60 each), tire rotation ($40), annual inspection ($35), plus the surprise $680 tire replacement and $240 brake job.
- **Registration:** $340/year in his state.

His car isn't costing him $385/month. It's costing him $870/month—$10,440/year. That's 24% of his take-home pay.

He's car-poor, and he didn't realize it until six months in.

Michael can't undo the purchase. But he can stop pretending the payment is the only cost. He added a "car costs" line to his budget: $385 payment + $190 insurance + $160 gas + $75/month sinking fund for maintenance + $30/month sinking fund for registration.

He also committed to two things: drive this car until it's paid off (no trading into something newer), and shop insurance annually. Switching companies saved him $35/month—$420/year for an hour of work.

The next car he buys, he'll calculate the *total* cost before signing anything.

Mia's Quarterly Tax Shock

Mia freelances full-time. She made $28,000 last year. She knew she'd owe taxes, but she figured she'd deal with it in April.

April came. She owed $6,100—federal income tax plus the 15.3% self-employment tax—plus $180 in penalties for not making quarterly estimated payments.

She didn't have $6,280. She set up an IRS payment plan, which comes with interest. Now she's making monthly payments on last year's taxes while trying to set aside money for this year's.

Nobody told her about quarterly taxes. W-2 employees have taxes withheld automatically. Freelancers are responsible for their own withholding, and the IRS expects you to pay *as you earn*—not in one lump sum in April.

Mia thought the money in her checking account was hers. It wasn't. 30% of it belonged to the IRS. She just didn't know it yet.

Now she has a separate savings account labeled "taxes." Every time a client pays her, she transfers 30% into that account the same day. She set calendar reminders for the quarterly due dates (April 15, June 15, September 15, January 15). She uses IRS Form 1040-ES to calculate and submit payments.

It's annoying. But it's less annoying than owing $6,100 she doesn't have.

Emma's Federal Benefits (And What She's Still Paying For)

Emma's federal job comes with benefits most private-sector workers don't get. Her health insurance options through FEHB are better than what most 24-year-olds have access to. She has a pension (FERS) in addition to her TSP. She gets federal holidays off.

But "good benefits" doesn't mean "free."

Her health insurance premium is $95/month (the government pays the rest). Her dental and vision are separate—$25/month combined. She opted into FEGLI (federal life insurance) at $18/month. She contributes 0.8% of her salary to FERS (the pension system)—about $45/month.

Her TSP contributions are 5% ($283/month) to get the full match. That's money she's choosing to invest, but it's still money that doesn't hit her checking account.

Total monthly deductions for benefits: $466. That's $5,592/year.

Emma's benefits are *good*. But they're not free. And when her coworkers talk about their "great federal salary," they're usually talking about the gross number—not the take-home after all the deductions.

She's fine with it. She knows what she's paying for. But it took her six months to stop being surprised by how much smaller her paycheck was than her salary.

Part 3: What Actually Changes Everything (Systems, Knowledge, and Agency)

The costs in this chapter aren't exciting. Nobody posts on Instagram about their renters insurance or their quarterly tax payment. But the difference between someone who plans for these costs and someone who gets blindsided by them is the difference between a budget that works and one that falls apart every other month.

The Shift from Reactive to Proactive

Jordan's first three months in her apartment were chaos. Every bill felt like a surprise. Every unexpected cost triggered a small panic. She was constantly moving money around, trying to cover things she hadn't planned for.

Then she sat down and made a list of every single cost she'd encountered. Rent, utilities, internet, renters insurance, household supplies, subscriptions, irregular expenses like her annual car registration and the $200 she spent on holiday gifts.

She built sinking funds—small monthly savings for predictable irregular expenses. $30/month for car registration and maintenance. $25/month for gifts and travel. $20/month for household replacements (the shower curtain that'll eventually need replacing, the light bulbs, the kitchen stuff that breaks).

It's not that the costs went away. It's that they stopped being emergencies.

Her budget went from "I hope I can cover everything this month" to "I know exactly what's coming and I've already set aside the money."

That shift—from reactive to proactive—changed everything.

Tyler's $500 Emergency Fund (And Why It Mattered)

When Tyler got the $2,400 medical bill, he had $500 in his emergency fund. It wasn't enough to cover the bill, but it was enough to give him options.

He didn't have to put the whole thing on a credit card at 22% APR. He could negotiate a payment plan, keep his emergency fund intact, and handle the $160/month without derailing his budget.

If he'd had $0 saved, the bill would've gone on the card. He would've paid interest. The $2,400 bill would've become $2,800, then $3,100, and he would've spent the next year digging out.

$500 didn't solve the problem. But it kept the problem from becoming a crisis.

That's what an emergency fund does. It's not about having enough to cover everything. It's about having enough to give yourself options.

Michael's Sinking Funds (And the End of Surprise Expenses)

Michael used to get hit with a $340 car registration bill every year and act like it was a surprise. It wasn't a surprise. It happened every year. He just hadn't planned for it.

Now he has a "car costs" sinking fund. $75/month for maintenance and repairs. $30/month for registration. When the bill comes, the money's already there.

He has a "life stuff" sinking fund. $40/month for the irregular expenses that used to blow up his budget—wedding gifts, travel for family events, the new work shoes he needs every 18 months, the annual subscription renewals.

The costs didn't go away. But they stopped feeling like emergencies.

Sinking funds are boring. They're also the difference between a budget that works and one that collapses every time something "unexpected" happens.

Emma's Proactive Research (And the Confidence That Comes With It)

Emma's good at this. When she started her federal job, she didn't just accept the default benefits. She researched. She compared health plans, calculated the total annual cost (premiums + expected out-of-pocket) for each option, checked the formulary to make sure her prescriptions were covered.

She picked a high-deductible plan and paired it with an HSA. She set her TSP contributions to get the full match and chose a target-date fund. She signed up for FEGLI life insurance because it's cheap and easy.

She didn't do this because she's naturally good with money. She did it because she knew that *not* understanding this stuff would cost her—in actual dollars and in stress.

The confidence she has now didn't come from being smart. It came from doing the research, asking the questions, and making informed decisions.

That's available to everyone. You just have to be willing to spend the time.

The Psychological Shift: From Shame to Agency

Jordan's first reaction to the move-in costs was shame. She felt like she'd failed. Like she should have known better. Like everyone else had figured this out and she was the only one struggling.

That's not true. Everyone struggles with this. The difference is that some people had parents who explained it, or friends who warned them, or enough financial cushion that the surprises didn't hurt.

Jordan didn't have that. But she has it now.

She knows what renters insurance covers. She knows to budget for the full cost of utilities, not just the average. She knows that the first month in a new place costs way more than one month's rent. She knows to ask about setup fees, deposits, and whether utilities are included before she signs a lease.

She's not behind. She's learning. And now that she knows, she can plan.

That shift—from "I should have known this" to "Now I know this"—is everything.

What You Actually Need to Know

You don't need to become obsessed with every line item. You don't need to track every dollar or optimize every decision. You just need to stop being surprised.

The basics:

- **Insurance exists to protect you from catastrophic loss.** Health, renters, auto—pay the premium so you don't get destroyed by the bill.
- **The first month in a new place costs 2–3x the rent.** Plan for it.
- **Cars cost way more than the payment.** Budget for insurance, gas, maintenance, and registration.

- **Freelancers owe quarterly taxes.** Set aside 30% of every payment the day it arrives.
- **Sinking funds turn irregular expenses into non-events.** Save monthly for things that hit annually.
- **Emergency funds give you options.** Even $500 matters.

None of this is complicated. It's just information nobody gave you.

Now you have it.

Your Move

- **Today:** Add up your actual monthly non-rent, non-food costs: insurance, phone, subscriptions, utilities, transportation. That's your real baseline.
- **This week:** Set up one sinking fund for a predictable irregular expense (car registration, holiday gifts, annual subscriptions).
- **This month:** If you're freelance, open a separate "taxes" savings account and start transferring 30% of every payment the day it arrives.

When It Goes Sideways

"I got a medical bill for $4,200 and I don't know what to do."

What happened: Tyler went to the ER after a workplace accident. He has insurance through his parents, but he's never used it for anything major. Three weeks later, a bill arrived for $4,200. His insurance paid $1,800 and left him with $2,400—his deductible plus coinsurance. He has $500 in his emergency fund.

Why it feels so bad: Tyler thought having insurance meant he was covered. He didn't know about deductibles, coinsurance, or out-of-pocket maximums. The bill felt like a betrayal—he'd done everything right, and he still owed thousands. He felt stupid for not knowing, and terrified he'd be sent to collections if he couldn't pay immediately.

Why it happens: Most people under 26 on their parents' insurance have never dealt with a real medical bill. They don't know how high-deductible plans work. And hospitals send bills that look urgent and final, even though they're almost always negotiable.

What to do:

First, breathe. Medical debt is different from credit card debt—it has negotiation options, interest-free payment plans, and protections that disappear the moment you convert it to credit card debt.

Second, request an itemized bill and compare it to the Explanation of Benefits (EOB) from insurance. Errors are common—duplicate charges, incorrect codes, charges for services not received.

Third, call the hospital's billing department. Ask about financial assistance or hardship programs. Many hospitals (especially nonprofits) have charity care for patients who qualify. Ask if they'll reduce the bill for a lump-sum payment, or set up an interest-free payment plan.

Tyler negotiated a 20% reduction and a 12-month payment plan—$160/month, no interest. His emergency fund stayed intact. The bill went from "financial catastrophe" to "annoying but manageable."

What not to do: Don't put it on a credit card. Don't ignore it. Don't assume the first bill is final.

"I just realized I haven't been paying quarterly taxes."

What happened: Mia earned $28,000 freelancing last year. She didn't know about quarterly estimated payments. She filed her taxes in April and owed $6,100—federal income tax plus the full 15.3% self-employment tax—plus $180 in underpayment penalties. She didn't have $6,280 sitting around.

Why it feels so bad: Mia thought the money in her checking account was hers. Finding out she owed $6,100 felt like being punished for something nobody told her about. She felt behind, irresponsible, and trapped—she's now paying off last year's taxes while trying to save for this year's.

Why it happens: Nobody tells freelancers about quarterly taxes. W-2 employees have taxes withheld automatically, so they never think about it. Freelancers are responsible for their own withholding, and the IRS expects you to pay as you earn—not in one lump sum in April. Mia spent the money she should have set aside because it was in her checking account and it felt like hers.

What to do:

Set up an IRS payment plan for the current debt. The interest rate is lower than credit cards, and the IRS is surprisingly reasonable if you're proactive. Don't ignore it—they have more collection power than any other creditor.

Going forward, open a separate savings account labeled "taxes." Transfer 30% of every freelance payment into it the day it arrives. Set calendar reminders for quarterly due dates (April 15, June 15, September 15, January 15). Use IRS Form 1040-ES to calculate and submit estimated payments.

It's annoying. But it's way less annoying than owing $6,100 you don't have.

What not to do: Don't skip the quarterly payments again this year because you're still paying off last year. That just doubles the problem. Don't ignore the IRS and hope it goes away.

"I had no idea my car would cost this much beyond the payment."

What happened: Michael's car payment is $385/month. He budgeted for that. What he didn't budget for: insurance ($190/month), gas ($160/month), maintenance ($75/month average), and registration ($340/year). His car is actually costing him $870/month—$10,440/year. That's 24% of his take-home pay.

Why it feels so bad: Michael thought he'd done the math. The payment felt manageable. But every month, something else hits—insurance, gas, an oil change, new tires. He feels trapped in a car he can't afford but can't get out of. He's underwater on the loan (owes more than the car is worth), so trading it in would just roll negative equity into a new loan and make the problem worse.

Why it happens: Car sellers and lenders focus on one number: the monthly payment. Everything else is invisible until the bills show up. Insurance varies by zip code, age, and driving record. Registration fees vary by state. Maintenance isn't optional—it's the cost of keeping the car running. And nobody tells you to calculate the *total* cost before you buy.

What to do:

Accept the real number and budget for it. Michael added a "car costs" line to his budget: $385 payment + $190 insurance + $160 gas + $75 maintenance sinking fund + $30 registration sinking fund = $840/month. That's higher than the recommended 15–20% of take-home, which means he's car-poor.

He can't undo the purchase, but he can: shop insurance annually (switching saved him $35/month), keep maintenance current to avoid bigger repair bills, and commit to driving this car until it's paid off rather than trading into something new.

The next car purchase, he'll calculate the total cost—payment + insurance + gas + maintenance + registration—before signing anything.

What not to do: Don't ignore the extra costs and let them blow up your budget every month. Don't skip maintenance to save money—a $60 oil change prevents a $4,000 engine repair. Don't trade in a car you're underwater on just because the payments feel heavy.

The expenses in this chapter aren't exciting. But the difference between someone who plans for these costs and someone who gets blindsided by them is the difference between a budget that works and one that falls apart every other month.

You don't need to become obsessed with every line item. You just need to stop being surprised.

Build the sinking funds. Know your real car cost. Understand how your insurance works. Set aside money for taxes if you're self-employed. Put a system in place so these expenses are boring—not emergencies.

Jordan's sitting on the floor of her apartment with $340 in her account was rock bottom. Six months later, she has a system. The costs didn't go away. But they stopped feeling like attacks.

That's the goal. Not to eliminate expenses—you can't. But to understand them, plan for them, and take away their power to derail you.

Now you know. Now you can plan.

Chapter 9: Big Purchases Without Big Regrets

"The best time to buy something is when you can afford it. The second best time is never." —Adapted wisdom

Michael got a text from a dealership. They were running a "loyalty event" — they wanted to get him into a newer model. Lower payment. Better features. All he had to do was come in.

He went. The salesman was friendly, showed him a loaded SUV, talked about the upgraded sound system and backup camera. Then they ran the numbers.

Michael's current car — the one he bought eighteen months ago — still had $14,200 on the loan. The car's trade-in value was $11,000. That meant he was $3,200 underwater. The dealership's solution: roll that $3,200 into the new loan. The SUV was $32,000. With the negative equity folded in, his new loan would be $35,200 — before taxes, fees, and the extended warranty they'd push in the finance office.

He'd be starting a brand new loan that was $3,200 in the hole on day one. And the cycle would start over.

Michael said he'd think about it. The salesman said the deal was only good today. Michael left anyway.

That was the right call. But Michael almost didn't make it. And thousands of people in his position sign that paperwork every day.

Big purchases — cars, apartments, eventually houses — involve more money than most of your other decisions combined. They shape your finances for years, sometimes decades. Get them right, and you've set yourself up. Get them wrong, and you're digging out for a long time.

Your Brain on Big Purchases

Before the specifics, you need to understand how your brain works against you in these situations — because every salesperson already does.

Anchoring

When Michael saw the $32,000 SUV, then looked at a $26,000 sedan, the sedan felt like a bargain. But could he actually afford a $26,000 car? His brain anchored to the first number and judged everything against it. Salespeople show you the expensive option first for exactly this reason.

The fix: decide what you can afford based on your income and budget before you walk into any showroom. Write that number down. Don't adjust it once you're there.

Monthly Payment Thinking

"It's only $400 a month!"

This is how people end up with cars, furniture, and electronics they can't afford. Sellers frame everything as a monthly payment because it sounds manageable. But $400/month for 72 months is $28,800 — plus interest.

The fix: calculate total cost, not monthly cost. Ask: "Would I pay $31,000 cash for this?" If the answer is no, the monthly payment doesn't change that.

The Emotional Trap

You imagine yourself in the apartment, driving the car, sitting on that couch. Once you've mentally moved in, walking away gets hard — even when the numbers say you should.

Salespeople know this. "Can you see yourself living here?" "Let's take it for a test drive!" Once you're emotionally attached, you'll rationalize almost any price.

The fix: research and set limits before you fall for anything specific. Be willing to walk away. There will always be another car, another apartment, another deal.

Lifestyle Creep

"I got a raise, so I deserve a nicer place."

Maybe. But upgrading every time your income increases is how people earn good money and still live paycheck to paycheck. Jordan got a $3,000 raise and immediately started browsing nicer apartments — which would have eaten the entire raise and then some.

The fix: when income goes up, increase your savings rate before your lifestyle.

Buying a Car

For most people, a car is the second-largest purchase they'll make. It's also one of the easiest places to make expensive mistakes.

Timing Matters

If you can plan ahead, November and December are typically the best months to buy. Dealers are rushing to hit annual, quarterly, and monthly quotas while clearing model-year inventory. That pressure works in your favor.

New vs. Used

A new car loses 20–30% of its value the moment you drive it off the lot. By year three, it's worth about half what you paid.

A 2–3 year old certified pre-owned (CPO) car gives you most of the reliability of new, often with remaining manufacturer warranty, at 30–40% less — because someone else already absorbed the steepest depreciation.

New vs. Used: The Real Math

	New Honda Accord	2-Year-Old Accord (25K miles)
Purchase price	$32,000	$21,000
Value after 3 years	~$19,000	~$14,500
Depreciation you pay	$13,000	$6,500
Warranty remaining	Full 3yr/36K	~1yr/11K (or CPO extension)

Tyler needs a car. He's been getting rides from his roommate and taking the bus, but it's limiting his ability to pick up extra shifts. He doesn't need a $32,000 Accord. He needs reliable transportation. A $7,000–$9,000 used Civic or Corolla with 80,000 miles and a clean history report gets him to work every day. That's the right car for his situation.

Unless you have very specific needs or money to burn, used is almost always the smarter financial move.

Dealer vs. Private Party

Buying from a dealer means easier financing, some consumer protections, and CPO options with warranties — but higher prices and pressure tactics. Best for people who want convenience or need financing.

Buying from a private party means lower prices and direct negotiation — but no warranty, financing is on you, and the paperwork is your responsibility. Best for cash buyers or people with pre-approved financing who are comfortable doing research.

Due diligence for any used car — don't skip any of these:

1. **Vehicle history report** — Carfax or AutoCheck ($25–$40). Shows accidents, title issues, odometer readings, service records. Non-negotiable.
2. **Pre-purchase inspection** — Pay a mechanic $100–$150 to inspect it before you buy. If the seller won't allow this, walk away.
3. **Title check** — Clean title only. Salvage, rebuilt, or flood titles mean the car was totaled and repaired. Hidden problems are almost guaranteed.

4. **VIN verification** — Dashboard VIN matches the title and registration. Mismatches mean potential fraud.
5. **Real test drive** — Highway and city. Test AC, heat, all windows, all lights. Listen for anything unusual.

How Much Car Can You Actually Afford?

The 20/4/10 Rule

Rule	What It Means
20% down	Minimum down payment
4-year loan max	48 months — not 60, not 72
10% of gross income	Maximum monthly payment

The Total Cost Rule: All car costs — payment, insurance, gas, maintenance — should stay under 15–20% of monthly take-home pay.

What This Looks Like for Each Character

Character	Monthly Take-Home	15–20% Car Budget	Realistic Car Payment (after insurance + gas)
Tyler	$2,210	$330–$440	$100–$180 (needs cheap, reliable)
Jordan	$3,120	$470–$625	$200–$350
Mia	$1,800–$3,400 (variable)	Budget on low months: $270–$360	$100–$200
Michael	$3,520	$530–$700	$250–$400 (currently at $840 total — car-poor)
Emma	$4,200	$630–$840	$300–$500

Michael's total car costs are $840/month — 24% of his take-home. He's car-poor. He can't undo the purchase, but he can shop insurance annually (switching saved him $35/month), keep up on maintenance to avoid bigger repair bills, and commit to driving this car until it's paid off rather than rolling into something new.

The Dealer Finance Office: Where They Really Get You

You negotiated the car price. You feel good. Then you're sent to the finance office.

This is where dealers make enormous margins. The person behind the desk will present add-ons as small monthly bumps — making each one sound trivial. They're not.

The Add-On Trap: What "Just a Few Dollars More" Actually Costs

Add-On	"Only..."	Over 72 Months
Extended warranty	$25/month	$1,800
Paint protection	$10/month	$720
Fabric coating	$8/month	$576
Gap insurance (dealer price)	$12/month	$864
Total	**$55/month**	**$3,960**

That $400/month payment becomes $455/month, and you've added nearly $4,000 to your total cost for products of questionable value. The $800 paint protection is fancy wax you could apply yourself for $30. The fabric coating is a $10 can of Scotchgard. Nitrogen in your tires? Air is already 78% nitrogen.

The move: Say no to everything in the finance office. Everything. You can always add coverage later after researching what it should cost. You can never un-buy something you signed for under pressure.

The one exception worth considering: gap insurance, if you're putting less than 20% down. But get quotes from your auto insurer first — it's usually much cheaper through them.

Negative Equity: Michael's Trap

This is worth its own section because it's one of the most common and expensive traps in car buying.

Michael owes $14,200 on a car worth $11,000. He's $3,200 underwater. Here's how it happened:

He put $1,500 down on a $22,000 car — less than 7% down. He took a 72-month loan. For the first three years of a 72-month loan, you're paying mostly interest. The car's value drops faster than the loan balance. The result: you owe more than the car is worth for most of the loan.

Michael's Negative Equity Timeline

Month	Loan Balance	Car Value	Equity
0 (purchase)	$20,500	$22,000	+$1,500
6	$19,200	$18,500	-$700
12	$17,800	$15,500	-$2,300
18 (now)	$14,200	$11,000	-$3,200
36	$10,500	$9,500	-$1,000
48	$6,800	$8,000	+$1,200
60	$3,400	$6,500	+$3,100

He won't have positive equity until around month 42. The dealer's offer to "get him into something new" would reset that clock entirely — he'd be $3,200 underwater on day one of a new loan, and the cycle would start over with an even larger balance.

If you're underwater on a car: - Keep driving it. Pay it down. Don't trade. - Make extra payments toward principal if possible — even $50/month accelerates the timeline. - Never roll negative equity into a new loan. You're just hiding the problem inside a bigger problem. - If the car is reliable, ride it past the loan payoff and enjoy the payment-free months.

Leasing: Rarely the Move

Leasing means renting a car for 2–3 years, then giving it back. You pay for the most expensive years of depreciation, deal with mileage limits, can't modify the car, and at the end you own nothing.

Leasing might make sense if you're self-employed and can deduct it as a business expense, or if you drive very low miles and keep cars in perfect condition. For most people, it's an expensive way to always have a car payment and never build equity.

Renting an Apartment

Housing is probably your biggest monthly expense. Getting this right has more impact on your finances than almost any other decision.

How Much Rent Can You Afford?

The traditional rule says 30% of gross income. The smarter rule: **25–30% of take-home pay**, including utilities.

Rent Affordability by Character

Character	Monthly Take-Home	25–30% Range	Current Rent	Verdict
Tyler	$2,210	$550–$665	$650 (with roommate)	Right at the edge
Jordan	$3,120	$780–$935	$1,250 (studio)	Over budget — 40% of take-home
Mia	~$2,400 avg	$600–$720	$800 (shared house)	Tight on slow months
Michael	$3,520	$880–$1,055	$1,100 (1BR)	31% — slightly over
Emma	$4,200	$1,050–$1,260	$1,350 (1BR)	32% — slightly over

Jordan's spending 40% of her take-home on rent. That's why her budget feels impossible every month — she's housing-rich and everything-else-poor. If she got a roommate and split a two-bedroom for $800 each, she'd free up $450/month. That's $5,400/year toward her student loans or investing.

In expensive cities, the 25–30% target might feel impossible. Your options: roommates, living further out, a smaller space, or increasing income. What you shouldn't do: spend 50% on rent and wonder why you can't save.

The True Cost of Moving In

Jordan's first-apartment surprise from Chapter 8 is worth repeating here because most people don't budget for it.

First Apartment: Total Move-In Costs

Expense	Cost Range
Security deposit (usually one month's rent)	$1,000–$1,500
First month's rent	$1,000–$1,500
Last month's rent (if required)	$1,000–$1,500
Application fees (multiple apps)	$75–$300
Moving costs	$200–$1,000
Furniture (basics only)	$1,500–$3,000
Utility setup fees	$50–$200
Household essentials	$200–$400
Total	**$5,000–$9,400**

For a $1,300/month apartment, Jordan needed roughly $5,000 before she even slept there one night. Plan for this. Start a "moving fund" sinking fund at least 6 months before you plan to move.

What to Ask Before Signing

Before you sign anything: What utilities are included? What's the lease term and early termination penalty? When was rent last raised, and what's typical for renewals? Is subletting allowed? What's the maintenance request process? How's cell service and internet? Ask about break-ins or crime in the area.

Red flags: pressure to sign immediately, refusal to show the actual unit you'd rent, bad reviews about management, high turnover, visible maintenance issues during the tour.

Roommates: The Math

Tyler already knows this — his $650 split is the only reason he can afford to live independently. The numbers make the case:

Arrangement	Monthly Cost
Studio	$1,400
1BR	$1,700
2BR split two ways	$1,100 each
3BR split three ways	$900 each

Roommates save $300–$600/month. Over a decade, that's $36,000–$72,000 that could go to debt payoff, investing, or building an emergency fund. The trade-off is privacy and potential drama. But financially, it's one of the biggest advantages available to young adults.

Buying a House (Eventually)

Homeownership is often presented as the ultimate financial goal. It can be a great move — but not always, and not for everyone.

When You're NOT Ready

Don't buy a house if you might move in the next 3–5 years (transaction costs eat your gains), don't have an emergency fund, carry high-interest debt, have an unstable job, or are buying only because "renting is throwing money away."

The "Renting Is Throwing Money Away" Myth

This is one of the most repeated and most misleading pieces of financial advice.

Yes, rent doesn't build equity. But homeownership costs that people forget about: mortgage interest (most of your early payments are interest, not equity), property taxes (1–2% of home value annually), homeowners insurance, maintenance (budget 1–

2% of home value per year), HOA fees ($100–$800+/month), and 5–6% transaction costs when you sell.

When you rent, your landlord absorbs all of that. You pay a predictable monthly amount, and when the furnace dies at 2 AM, it's their problem.

Renting isn't "throwing money away" any more than buying food or paying for transportation. You're paying for a thing you need. The question is whether buying or renting is more cost-effective for your specific situation. The New York Times "Is It Better to Rent or Buy?" calculator is one of the best free tools for running those numbers.

When Buying Makes Sense

Consider buying if you plan to stay 5–7+ years, have stable income, have 10–20% for a down payment (ideally 20% to avoid PMI), have a separate emergency fund, and the total monthly cost is comparable to renting.

The Numbers

Down payment: traditionally 20%, but 3–5% is possible with certain loans. Less than 20% means paying PMI ($100–$300+/month) until you reach 20% equity.

Closing costs: 2–5% of the home price. On a $300,000 home, that's $6,000–$15,000 on top of your down payment. These cover the loan origination fee, appraisal, inspection, title insurance, attorney fees, escrow deposits, and recording fees. Some are negotiable — ask your agent and lender.

Affordability rule: Keep total housing costs (mortgage + taxes + insurance + HOA) under 28% of gross income. If you earn $75,000/year ($6,250/month gross), that's about $1,750/month. With current rates, that might support a $250,000–$300,000 home depending on your area.

Lenders will approve you for more house than you should buy. The approval ceiling is not a target.

Don't Skip the Home Inspection

A home inspection costs $300–$500 and takes 2–4 hours. It can save you tens of thousands. The inspector checks structural integrity, roof condition, electrical and plumbing systems, HVAC, water damage, mold, exterior drainage, and insulation.

You can negotiate repairs, negotiate a price reduction, or walk away using your inspection contingency. Depending on the property, you might also need specialized inspections: pest/termite, radon, sewer line scope, or well and septic.

Never buy a house without an inspection. The $400 you save by skipping it is nothing compared to the $15,000 foundation repair you didn't see coming.

Hidden Costs of Homeownership

Budget for maintenance (1–2% of home value annually), big-ticket repairs that will eventually happen (roof: $10,000–$25,000; HVAC: $5,000–$15,000; water heater: $1,000–$3,000), yard care, higher utilities, and the improvements you'll convince yourself you "need."

Homeownership is not passive. It's a part-time job you pay for.

First-Time Buyer Programs

If you're considering buying, look into FHA loans (3.5% down, flexible credit), VA loans (0% down, no PMI for veterans), USDA loans (0% down for rural areas), state and local first-time buyer programs, and employer assistance programs.

These programs can make buying more accessible — but don't let them convince you to buy before you're ready.

HUD-approved homebuyer education courses (available through HUD.gov, 4–8 hours, free or under $100) are required by some programs and worth taking regardless.

The Big Purchase Checklist

Before any major purchase, run through this:

Can you actually afford it? Not "can you make the payments" — does it fit comfortably in your budget while still allowing you to save and handle emergencies?

What's the total cost? Interest, insurance, maintenance, opportunity cost. The sticker price is just the beginning.

What are you giving up? Every dollar here is a dollar not spent elsewhere. Is this worth more than the alternative?

Are you deciding emotionally? Sleep on it. 48–72 hours minimum. If you're being pressured to decide today, that's a red flag.

Have you shopped around? The first option is rarely the best deal.

What's your exit strategy? For a car: can you sell it without being underwater? For an apartment: what's the lease-break penalty? For a house: how long to break even after selling costs (typically 5–7 years)? A purchase that looks great until you realize you're trapped isn't great.

Big purchases shape your financial life for years. The goal isn't to never buy anything nice — it's to make informed choices that fit your actual situation, not impulse decisions you'll regret.

Take your time. Do the math. Be willing to walk away.

Your Move

- **Today:** If you have a car, calculate your real monthly cost: payment + insurance + gas + maintenance + registration. That's your actual car number.

- **This week:** If you're apartment hunting, calculate the true move-in cost (first/last/deposit + furniture + setup fees). It's probably 2–3x the rent.
- **Before any big purchase:** Run the total cost, not the monthly payment. If a salesperson only talks in monthly numbers, that's a red flag.

When It Goes Sideways

"The dealer wants to roll my negative equity into a new loan."

What happened: Michael's been making payments on his car for eighteen months. He still owes $14,200 on a car worth $11,000 — he's $3,200 underwater. The dealership texted him about a "loyalty event" and offered to get him into a newer SUV. Their plan: trade in his current car, absorb the $3,200 gap by adding it to the new loan. The new loan would start at $35,200 for a $32,000 vehicle. His monthly payment would actually go up, and he'd be even deeper underwater from day one.

Why it happens: Dealers make money on transactions — every sale, every trade, every financing deal generates profit. They don't care about your equity position. Rolling negative equity is one of the most profitable plays in the car business because it creates a larger loan (more interest revenue for the lender, bigger commission for the dealer) and locks you into a longer repayment cycle. The pitch sounds helpful: "We'll take care of your old loan." What they mean is: "We'll hide your old debt inside a bigger debt."

What to do: Say no and keep driving. Michael's car is eighteen months old and presumably reliable — he doesn't need a new one. He should focus on paying down the loan until he has positive equity (around month 42 at his current pace). If he can add even $50–$100/month toward principal, he'll get there faster. Meanwhile, he shops insurance annually to lower costs and keeps up on maintenance to extend the car's life. The goal: pay it off, then enjoy the payment-free months while saving for a proper down payment on his next car.

What not to do: Roll the negative equity. Ever. You're not solving a problem — you're compounding it. Also don't extend to a longer loan term to make the payment "work." A 72 or 84-month loan on a depreciating asset guarantees you'll be underwater for years. And don't fall for "your payment will only go up $30/month" framing — do the total cost math. Michael's $30/month increase over 72 months is $2,160 in additional payments, on top of the $3,200 in buried negative equity, on top of the higher purchase price. The real cost of that "deal" is north of $5,000.

"I found an apartment I love but it's $400 over my budget."

Jordan found a one-bedroom with in-unit laundry, a balcony, and a short walk to work. Rent is $1,650/month. Her budget says $1,250 max. She's already mentally decorated the living room.

So what do you do?

The math first: $400/month is $4,800/year. That's her entire annual student loan overpayment budget. Or a fully funded Roth IRA contribution. Or the difference between an emergency fund that grows and one that stalls. The apartment isn't $400 more per month — it's $4,800 less per year toward every other financial goal she has.

Jordan tells herself she'll cut back on eating out to cover the gap. She won't. Almost nobody does. The budget cuts people promise during apartment hunting are the financial equivalent of "I'll start going to the gym Monday." You sign the lease, the excitement fades, and you're spending $1,650 on rent *plus* your normal spending, wondering why your savings account hasn't moved.

Walk away. If $1,250 doesn't get her something she likes, she should look at roommate situations or adjacent neighborhoods —

not stretch into a lease that wrecks her plan. The apartment that fits your budget and is fine will always beat the apartment that's perfect but keeps you broke.

The thing nobody mentions: Landlords know the emotional hook works. That's why they stage apartments, why they schedule viewings when the light is best, and why they pressure you to "apply today before it's gone." Treat apartment hunting like car buying — decide your number before you walk in, and don't let the experience talk you out of it.

"My parents are pressuring me to buy a house, but I'm not ready."

What happened: Emma's parents — both military, both homeowners since their mid-twenties — keep asking when she's going to stop "wasting money on rent." They bought their first house with a VA loan at 24. They don't understand why Emma, with her stable federal job and good credit, is still renting at the same age. Her mom sent her Zillow listings three times last month.

Why it happens: Generational expectations. Emma's parents bought in a market where home prices were lower relative to income, interest rates were different, and the VA loan made the down payment a non-issue. They're not wrong that homeownership worked for them. But the math has changed — median home prices have outpaced wage growth significantly, and the "always buy" advice doesn't account for Emma's $28,000 in student loans, her desire to stay flexible for potential transfers, or the fact that she's only been in her position for two years.

What to do: Emma runs the numbers honestly. Her rent is $1,350/month. A comparable home in her area would cost roughly $350,000. With 5% down ($17,500), her mortgage payment plus taxes, insurance, and PMI would be around $2,600/month — nearly double her rent. She'd also need to drain her emergency fund for the down payment and closing costs. The math doesn't work yet. She can show her parents the numbers, thank them for caring, and explain that she's building toward homeownership on a timeline that makes financial sense — not one that puts her in a bind.

What not to do: Buy a house to make your parents happy. Also, don't assume you're "behind" because your parents bought at 24 in a different era, or because friends your age are buying — they might have family money for a down payment, a partner splitting costs, or they didn't read this book and are about to learn some expensive lessons. Emma's plan — pay down student loans, build savings, contribute to TSP, and buy when the numbers actually work — is the smarter move, even if it doesn't match her parents' timeline.

Every big purchase in this chapter has the same underlying pattern: the emotional pull is immediate, but the financial impact plays out over years. The car payment that "fits your budget" until you add insurance, gas, and maintenance. The apartment that's "only" $400 more. The house your parents think you should buy because they bought one at your age in a different economy.

The move is always the same. Run the real numbers — not the monthly payment, the total cost. Compare what you'd spend against what you'd lose in opportunity. And make the decision with a calculator, not a daydream.

Your future self will thank you. Probably while driving a paid-off car to an apartment that left room in the budget for a life.

Chapter 10: Protecting Future You

> *"Someone is sitting in the shade today because someone planted a tree a long time ago." —Warren Buffett*

Emma has a will. She's 24. Her coworkers think that's paranoid. She thinks it's practical.

She set it up three months after starting her federal job — used an online service for $150, named her younger sister as the person who'd get her savings and TSP balance, designated her mom as her healthcare proxy, and filed a financial power of attorney naming her dad. She had two coworkers who weren't named in the will witness her signing, then took it to a UPS Store notary to make it official. The whole thing took two hours on a Saturday afternoon and $15 for the notary.

Tyler, Jordan, Mia, and Michael have none of this. No will. No healthcare directive. No power of attorney. No beneficiary designations beyond whatever they accidentally clicked during enrollment. They're not unusual — most people in their twenties don't have these documents. But "most people" isn't a plan.

This chapter covers the boring, uncomfortable, critically important stuff: the documents you need, the protections you should set up, and the scams you need to recognize — all while it's easy, not after it's urgent.

The Documents Every Adult Needs

Estate planning isn't for old people with money. These documents protect you and the people you care about right now.

Will

A will says what happens to your stuff when you die. Without one, your state decides — and their default rules might not match what you'd want.

Why you need one even if you're young and broke: If you have anything of value — a car, savings, even sentimental items — a will says who gets it. If you have pets, a will designates who takes them. If you have kids, a will names their guardian (without one, a court decides). And it makes things dramatically easier for your family during an already terrible time.

What happens without one: Each state has intestate succession rules. Generally: spouse, then children, then parents, then siblings. But an unmarried partner gets nothing by default — even after twenty years together. Close friends get nothing. That estranged family member you haven't spoken to in a decade might inherit everything.

How to get one:

Option	Cost	Best For
Online services (Trust & Will, LegalZoom, Rocket Lawyer)	\$100–\$300	Simple situations — single, no kids, straightforward assets
Estate planning attorney	\$300–\$1,000+	Blended families, significant assets, business ownership, anything complex

What makes a will valid: State laws vary, but generally you need your signature plus two disinterested witnesses (people who aren't beneficiaries) who watch you sign and then sign themselves. Some states require notarization. Some states now accept electronic wills with e-signatures and remote video witnessing. Online services typically walk you through your state's requirements.

An unsigned will in a drawer does nothing. Sign it, witness it, store it somewhere your family can find it.

Healthcare Directive (Living Will)

This document states your wishes for medical care if you can't speak for yourself — whether you want life-sustaining treatment, your pain management preferences, and your organ donation wishes.

This isn't morbid. It's the opposite — it prevents your family from having to guess what you'd want while arguing with each other and medical staff during the worst moment of their lives.

Healthcare Power of Attorney

This names someone to make medical decisions for you if you can't make them yourself. Your healthcare agent can consent to or refuse treatment, access your medical records, and communicate with doctors on your behalf.

Choose someone you trust completely, who will follow your wishes even if they disagree, who can handle pressure, and who lives close enough to be physically present. Tell them you're naming them and discuss your wishes in advance.

HIPAA Authorization

Often overlooked but important. HIPAA protects your medical privacy — which is great until someone you trust needs your medical information and can't get it. A HIPAA authorization gives specific people permission to access your records and speak with your providers. Without it, even a spouse or parent may be blocked from getting basic information about your condition.

Many healthcare POA forms include HIPAA language, but not all. You can sign a standalone HIPAA authorization form (free online) and give copies to your doctors' offices.

Financial Power of Attorney

This names someone to handle your finances if you can't — paying bills, managing accounts, filing taxes, dealing with insurance.

Springing power of attorney only takes effect if you become incapacitated. **Durable** takes effect immediately and continues through incapacity. For most young adults, springing makes sense — it's only there if you need it. Choose carefully. This person will have access to your money.

Where to Keep These Documents

Physical copies in a fireproof safe, with your attorney, or with a trusted family member. Note: safe deposit boxes can be hard to access immediately after a death. **Digital copies** scanned and stored in password-protected cloud storage. **Tell people** – your healthcare agent, financial agent, and close family should know these documents exist and where to find them.

The "Future You" Checklist

Document	What It Does	Do You Have It?
Will	Says who gets your stuff	☐
Healthcare directive	States your medical wishes	☐
Healthcare power of attorney	Names your medical decision-maker	☐
HIPAA authorization	Lets trusted people access medical info	☐
Financial power of attorney	Names your financial decision-maker	☐
Copies stored safely + someone knows where	–	☐

Emma handled all of this in one Saturday. It cost $165 and two hours. That's cheaper than a decent dinner out and worth infinitely more.

Beneficiary Designations: The Thing Everyone Forgets

Here's something that catches people off guard: beneficiary designations on accounts override your will.

If your will says "everything goes to my partner" but your 401(k) beneficiary is still your ex from three years ago, your ex gets the 401(k). The will doesn't matter for that account.

Accounts that have beneficiary designations: 401(k) and workplace retirement plans, IRAs, TSP, life insurance policies, HSAs, and bank accounts (with a "payable on death" or POD designation) and brokerage accounts (with a "transfer on death" or TOD designation).

POD and TOD: Beneficiaries for Everyday Accounts

Most people know retirement accounts have beneficiaries. What many don't realize is that you can add beneficiaries to regular checking, savings, and brokerage accounts too.

Payable on Death (POD) for bank accounts and **Transfer on Death (TOD)** for investment accounts work the same way: the account functions normally while you're alive; when you die, the beneficiary shows a death certificate and ID to claim the funds. The money bypasses probate entirely — no waiting, no court.

This matters because probate can take months or years and cost thousands in legal fees. Setting up POD/TOD is free and takes ten minutes.

What to do now:

1. List every account that has (or could have) a beneficiary
2. Log in and check who's currently listed
3. Update as needed
4. Name contingent beneficiaries (backups in case your primary dies first)
5. Add POD/TOD to accounts that don't have beneficiaries yet
6. Review annually or after any major life change

Emma's TSP beneficiary is her sister. Her HYSA has a POD designation naming her mom. Michael hasn't checked his 401(k) beneficiary since enrollment — he vaguely remembers listing his mom, but he's not sure. That needs to be certain, not vague.

Common mistakes: Naming your estate as beneficiary (creates tax problems for retirement accounts), forgetting to update after major life changes, not naming contingent beneficiaries, and assuming your will covers everything.

Identity Protection

Identity theft can wreck your finances and take months to resolve. A few steps dramatically reduce your risk.

Credit Freezes: The Best Free Protection

A credit freeze restricts access to your credit report, making it much harder for someone to open accounts in your name. It's free, effective, and barely anyone does it.

You freeze your credit at each of the three bureaus. When someone applies for credit in your name, the lender can't pull your report — application denied. You temporarily lift the freeze when you legitimately need to apply.

How to freeze:

Bureau	Where to Freeze
Equifax	equifax.com/personal/credit-report-services/credit-freeze
Experian	experian.com/freeze
TransUnion	transunion.com/credit-freeze

Each bureau gives you a PIN to lift the freeze. Store these PINs securely. Lifting is easy — often online, and you can specify how long (a few days is usually enough for a credit application, apartment check, or new phone plan).

Tyler should freeze his credit now. He's building credit for the first time (Chapter 6), and a freeze protects that clean slate from being hijacked before he even gets started. Everyone else should too — Mia especially, since she already had medical collections she didn't know about. A freeze costs nothing and takes five minutes per bureau.

Password and Account Security

Use strong, unique passwords. A password manager (Bitwarden, 1Password) makes this manageable. Never reuse passwords across accounts. Your email password is the most critical — if someone gets into your email, they can reset passwords for everything.

Enable two-factor authentication on financial accounts, email, and social media. Use an authenticator app (Google Authenticator, Authy) rather than SMS when possible — SIM swapping attacks can intercept text messages.

Monitor your accounts. Set up transaction alerts — many banks let you set alerts for any transaction over a certain amount. A $1 threshold catches fraud fast.

Secure your mail. Identity theft still happens through stolen mail. Consider a locking mailbox or use USPS Informed Delivery (free — emails you images of incoming mail).

Protect your Social Security number. Don't carry the card. Don't give out your SSN unless absolutely necessary — many places that ask don't actually need it.

Paid Identity Theft Services

Services like LifeLock and Aura charge $10–$30+/month. The reality: you can monitor your credit for free (AnnualCreditReport.com, Credit Karma), credit freezes are more effective at prevention, and most services alert you after fraud has occurred rather than preventing it.

For most people, the free approach wins: credit freezes + free monitoring + good security practices. Save the $200+/year for your emergency fund.

Paid services might make sense if you've already been a victim or want the convenience of recovery assistance if something happens.

If Your Identity Is Stolen

Act fast: place a fraud alert on your credit reports, review all three reports for accounts you don't recognize, report to the FTC at IdentityTheft.gov (they'll create a personalized recovery plan), file a police report, contact affected companies to dispute and close fraudulent accounts, change compromised passwords, and monitor closely for months afterward. The FTC site walks you through every step and generates dispute letters for you.

Insurance Gaps to Close

Chapter 8 covered the basics. Here are protections that specifically guard your future.

Umbrella Insurance

An umbrella policy provides extra liability coverage beyond your auto and renters/homeowners insurance — it kicks in when you've exhausted those limits. One bad car accident with injuries could result in a judgment for hundreds of thousands. Umbrella policies run $200–$400/year for $1 million in coverage.

For young adults just starting out, this might not be a priority yet. But as you build wealth, it becomes important. Keep it on your radar.

Disability Insurance (Revisited)

Your ability to earn income is your most valuable asset. You're more likely to become disabled during your working years than to die — yet most people skip disability coverage.

Emma's federal FERS provides a disability retirement benefit as a last resort, but it requires 18 months of service and pays less than full salary. Mia has zero disability protection as a gig worker — one injury that keeps her from driving or designing and her income drops to zero overnight. If your employer offers long-term disability, take it. If you're self-employed or in a physically demanding job without coverage, consider an individual policy.

Annual Coverage Review

Life changes. Insurance should change with it. Each year: Has your income changed? Have you acquired valuable property? Have you gotten married or had kids? Have you bought a home or car? Set a calendar reminder — do it when you file taxes or on your birthday.

Financial Scams to Watch For

Scammers target young adults because they're often new to managing money. Knowing the patterns saves you.

Get-Rich-Quick Schemes

If someone promises huge returns with little effort, they're lying. Every version: "I made $10,000 last month working from home" (MLM — you'll lose money), "guaranteed 20% returns" (fraud or undisclosed risk), "secret strategy the banks don't want you to know" (there are no secrets). Wealth is built slowly through boring strategies. Anyone selling shortcuts is selling lies.

Pyramid Schemes and MLMs

Multi-level marketing companies technically sell products, but the real money comes from recruiting. Red flags: emphasis on recruiting over selling, required inventory purchases, unrealistic income claims, pressure to recruit friends and family. Check the company's income disclosure statement — most participants make little or nothing.

Crypto and Investment Scams

Crypto has legitimate uses, but it's highly speculative and a massive scam magnet. Even seasoned investors with decades of experience rarely put more than 5% of their total invested capital into crypto — and they treat that 5% as money they might never see again. If the people with the most knowledge and experience are capping their exposure that low, a beginner going all-in on a coin their coworker recommended is not investing. It's gambling.

Pump-and-dump schemes, fake exchanges, "guaranteed" crypto returns (no such thing), and romance scams involving crypto are all common. Tyler's coworker from Chapter 7 who hypes crypto gains is one thing — a stranger in your DMs with investment advice is another.

Rules: only invest what you can afford to lose completely, cap crypto at 5% of your portfolio maximum, use established exchanges, and never send crypto to someone you met online.

Imposter and Phishing Scams

The IRS will never call demanding immediate payment, threaten arrest, or ask for gift cards. Your bank won't call asking for your full account number or password. Real employers don't ask you to pay for training or deposit checks and send money back. If someone contacts you claiming to be from a trusted institution, hang up and call the number on your card or statement.

Romance Scams

Someone you meet online develops a relationship. Eventually, they need money — emergency, business opportunity, can't meet until some financial issue is resolved. They might use AI-generated photos. They always have an excuse for why they can't video chat or meet in person. They fell in love fast.

The rule: never send money to someone you haven't met in person, no matter how real it feels.

The Universal Defense

Slow down — scammers create urgency. Verify independently — go to the website directly, never click links. Talk to someone before any major financial decision — scammers isolate their victims. Google "[company name] + scam" before giving money to anyone. Trust your gut.

If you've been scammed: report to the FTC (reportfraud.ftc.gov) and your state attorney general. Contact your bank immediately if you sent money via wire transfer. Follow the identity theft steps above if you gave out personal information.

Building Your Financial Safety System

Think of everything in this chapter as layers:

Your Financial Protection Layers

Layer	What It Does	Status
Emergency fund	Cash for immediate crises	Built in Chapter 4
Insurance	Protection against catastrophic loss	Covered in Chapter 8, gaps closed here
Legal documents	Ensures your wishes are followed	Will, POA, healthcare directive
Identity protection	Prevents others from destroying what you've built	Freezes, passwords, monitoring
Beneficiary designations	Assets go where you want	All accounts reviewed and updated

Each layer reinforces the others. An emergency fund without insurance still leaves you exposed to catastrophe. Insurance without legal documents means your family struggles even if there's money. Legal documents without updated beneficiaries means assets go to the wrong people.

Build all the layers. Review them annually. Update when life changes.

Your Move

- **Today:** Freeze your credit at all three bureaus if you haven't already. Fifteen minutes.
- **This week:** Check your beneficiaries on every account that has them—401(k), TSP, IRA, life insurance, bank accounts. Update anything that's outdated.

- **This month:** Complete at least a healthcare directive and financial power of attorney. Online services cost $100–$300. A Saturday afternoon and the cost of a nice dinner—for documents that could save your family thousands and months of stress.

When It Goes Sideways

"Someone opened a credit card in my name."

What happened: Mia checked her credit report (something she started doing quarterly after learning about her medical collections in Chapter 6) and found a credit card she'd never opened. It had a $3,400 balance and was 60 days past due. Someone had used her Social Security number — likely from a data breach she didn't know about — to open the account four months ago. Her credit score had already dropped 85 points.

Why it happens: Data breaches are constant. Your Social Security number, date of birth, and address have probably been exposed in at least one breach already. Criminals buy this information in bulk and open accounts, sometimes waiting months before using them. Mia didn't have a credit freeze — she didn't know it was an option until now.

What to do: Mia freezes her credit at all three bureaus immediately to prevent more accounts from being opened. She files a fraud alert with one bureau (it automatically applies to all three). She reports to the FTC at IdentityTheft.gov, which generates a personalized recovery plan and dispute letters. She files a police report for documentation. She disputes the fraudulent account with both the credit card company and the credit bureaus in writing. She changes passwords on all financial accounts and enables two-factor authentication everywhere. The fraudulent account and the 85-point drop should be removed once the dispute is resolved — typically 30–90 days.

What not to do: Ignore it and hope it goes away. It won't — it'll get worse. Also, don't call the number on the fraudulent account's statement (it might connect you to the scammer). Don't pay any portion of the fraudulent balance. And don't skip the police report — you may need it for disputes, and it creates a legal record.

"My roommate died and I can't access any of their accounts to pay shared bills."

What happened: Tyler's roommate was in a serious car accident and passed away. They shared a lease, split utilities, and had a joint streaming account. Tyler couldn't access his roommate's bank account to cover the remaining utility bills, couldn't get the landlord to remove the roommate from the lease without a death certificate and legal process, and spent weeks in limbo trying to sort out shared financial obligations while grieving.

Why it happens: Most young adults don't think about what happens to shared financial obligations if something happens to one person. No power of attorney was in place, no will existed, and shared accounts weren't structured to handle this situation. The default legal process for accessing a deceased person's assets involves probate — which can take months.

What to do: Tyler contacts the landlord immediately to explain the situation and negotiate the lease — most landlords will work with surviving tenants. He contacts utility companies with a copy of the death certificate to remove the roommate's name. For shared expenses he's paid in the interim, he keeps receipts in case the roommate's estate reimburses shared costs. Going forward, Tyler sets up his own documents — will, healthcare directive, POA — so his own roommate or family won't face the same confusion. He also adds POD designations to his own accounts.

What not to do: Assume someone else will handle it. Also, don't access the deceased person's individual accounts — even with good intentions, using someone else's login credentials or bank account after death can create legal problems. Let the legal process work, even when it's frustratingly slow.

"I fell for a scam and sent $800 to someone online."

Jordan matched with someone on a dating app. Three weeks of long messages, voice calls, plans to meet up. Then the person said they were stuck — wallet stolen while traveling, couldn't access their bank, could Jordan send $800 via Venmo to cover a hotel and flight home? She sent it. The profile disappeared the next day.

Here's what you need to know: the $800 is almost certainly gone. Venmo transactions to strangers are nearly impossible to reverse. That's the bad news.

The good news is that what Jordan does *next* actually matters. Report to the FTC at reportfraud.ftc.gov. Report to the dating app so they can pull the profile. File a police report — the cops won't recover $800, but documentation matters if this person is running the same play on dozens of people. Contact Venmo's fraud department. And review whether she shared personal information during those three weeks — address, workplace, financial details — that could be used for further targeting.

The hardest part isn't the money. It's the embarrassment. Jordan didn't send cash to a stranger — she sent it to someone she thought she knew. That's exactly what the scammer counted on, and it's why these schemes work on smart people. Romance scams cost Americans over $1.3 billion a year. Jordan isn't gullible. She's human.

One rule going forward: Never send money to someone you haven't met in person. Not Venmo, not Zelle, not gift cards, not crypto. If someone you've only met online has a financial emergency, they have other people in their life who can help. If they don't — that's a red flag, not a reason to open your wallet.

This chapter covers the stuff nobody wants to think about — wills at 24, identity theft, scams, the possibility that something bad happens to someone you share bills with. It's not fun. But the people who handle these situations best aren't the ones who predicted them. They're the ones who set up the paperwork, froze their credit, and organized their accounts *before* anything went wrong.

Twenty minutes setting up a credit freeze. An afternoon getting your documents in order. A conversation with someone you trust about where to find things if something happens to you.

That's it. That's the whole chapter distilled into three moves. Everything else is details.

Chapter 11: Social Media and Your Financial Health

"Comparison is the thief of joy." —Theodore Roosevelt (who, thankfully, never had to deal with Instagram)

Jordan's Weekend

Friday night, 9:47 PM. Jordan's on her couch after a long week, scrolling Instagram with no particular intention. Just decompressing.

Then she sees it: her college friend Sarah's story. Rooftop dinner. New outfit—something flowy and expensive-looking. Cocktails with a view of the city. The caption: "Finally treating myself."

Jordan feels it immediately. Not jealousy exactly. More like she's missing something. Like everyone else got an invitation to a life she's not living.

She keeps scrolling. Another friend posted a clothing haul from a brand Jordan follows. The friend's trying things on, laughing, saying "I'm obsessed" about a jacket. Jordan clicks through to the brand's page. The jacket is $89. She adds it to cart.

She tells herself she'll think about it.

She buys it four minutes later.

Saturday morning, Jordan wakes up and checks her phone. Her Instagram feed looks different. It's full of vacation content now—beaches, resort pools, "weekend getaway" posts. She didn't follow any of these accounts yesterday. But she'd lingered on Sarah's rooftop story for maybe thirty seconds last night. Double-tapped it. The algorithm noticed.

She scrolls through the vacation posts. Stops on one: a couple in Tulum, perfect lighting, the kind of photo that makes you feel like your own life is happening in black and white. She doesn't know these people. But she wants what they have.

An influencer she follows—someone with 400K followers who posts "day in my life" content—just dropped a "my favorite products this month" post. Skincare, a water bottle, a planner, the jacket Jordan just bought yesterday. The influencer says it's all stuff she "genuinely loves."

Jordan doesn't know the influencer gets a commission every time someone clicks her links. She doesn't know this post is sponsored content, even without the #ad tag. She just knows someone she admires uses these things, and maybe if she had them too, her life would feel more put together.

By noon, Jordan's at brunch with coworkers. She wasn't planning to go—she'd budgeted for a quiet weekend—but everyone else was going and the group chat made it sound fun. She orders the avocado toast and a mimosa. $45 with tip.

Saturday afternoon, she's back on her phone. Three people she follows posted about an upcoming concert tour. She's not even sure she likes the artist that much, but the posts make it seem like everyone's going. Like if she doesn't go, she'll be the only one who missed it.

She buys two tickets. $175.

Monday morning, she checks her bank account. She'd had $180 left for discretionary spending this month, and she was planning to put anything extra toward her student loans.

The jacket: $89. Brunch: $45. Concert tickets: $175. A few smaller purchases she barely remembers—coffee, a book, a subscription box she signed up for during a targeted ad. Total: $340.

She didn't decide to spend $340. She reacted. To a feed. To a weekend of scrolling that felt passive but wasn't. Every post, every story, every ad—it was designed to make her feel like she was missing something. And the algorithm learned exactly what would make her click.

Jordan sits on her couch, staring at her phone, and realizes: I'm not in control of this. The feed is.

Emma and the Algorithm

Emma's been casually following a few luxury apartment accounts on Instagram. Not because she's moving—she's not—but because she likes the aesthetic. Clean lines, natural light, plants in every corner. Aspirational, but harmless. Or so she thought.

She scrolls one night, double-taps a few posts. Lingers on one for maybe thirty seconds, imagining what it would be like to live somewhere that bright and open. She doesn't think much of it.

The next day, her entire feed has shifted.

Luxury apartments everywhere. Furniture brands she's never heard of. Home decor ads. "Apartment tour" reels from influencers showing off spaces that cost $3,500/month. Every third post is the same aesthetic, the same vibe, the same unspoken message: this is what your life should look like.

Emma notices something else: she's not just seeing apartments anymore. She's seeing the furniture to fill them. The art for the walls. The rugs, the lighting, the plants. Each post leads to another. Each double-tap teaches the algorithm what she wants.

Except she didn't want any of this yesterday.

She sits with her phone in her hand and realizes: it's not showing me what I'm interested in. It's showing me what will make me want to spend.

The algorithm isn't recommending. It's selling.

She thinks about her TSP contributions, her emergency fund, her plan to buy a house in a few years. Then she thinks about how many times this week she almost clicked "buy now" on something she saw in her feed.

She opens her settings and unfollows fifteen accounts. Not because they're bad. Because they're working exactly as designed—and she's the product.

Michael and the Crypto Guru

Michael's in a group chat with four guys from college. They talk a few times a week—mostly memes, sports, plans that never happen.

Then one of them, Derek, posts a screenshot. A crypto portfolio. Up 40% in a month.

Michael replies: "Damn, nice."

Two days later, Derek posts again. A photo of a Rolex on his wrist. Caption: "When you bet on yourself." Then another post: his new apartment. High-rise, floor-to-ceiling windows, the kind of place that costs $2,800/month minimum.

Michael's impressed. He asks how Derek figured this out. Derek sends links—TikTok accounts. Finance influencers. Young guys, mid-twenties, showing off cars, watches, stacks of cash. They talk about crypto, day trading, "beating the system." They all have courses for sale. $299. $499. "Limited spots available."

Michael watches a few videos. They're confident. They make it sound easy. They show their gains—screenshots of portfolios up 60%, 80%, 120% in a year.

Then Michael notices something.

Every single one of them is selling a course. The cars, the watches, the apartments—they're not proof the strategy works. They're proof the course sells.

He goes back to Derek's posts. Looks closer. Derek's not just sharing wins anymore. He's recruiting. Three of his last five posts mention "learning the strategy" or "if you're serious about this, DM me."

Michael realizes: Derek makes money whether the coin goes up or down. He makes it from people like Michael buying in.

He thinks back to Chapter 7. Tyler's coworker at the warehouse, the one who wouldn't shut up about crypto. Same energy. Same flexing. Same "get in now before it's too late" urgency.

Michael closes TikTok. He's not buying a course. And he's not buying the coin.

The influencer lifestyle isn't proof. It's the product.

Mia and the Treat Yourself Trap

Mia's doing her monthly budget review—something she started after Chapter 3—and she's looking at her bank statement from the last three weeks.

She sees it immediately: a pattern she didn't notice in real time.

$12 app subscription. $9 meditation app. $15 subscription box. $8 coffee. $22 book. $18 candle. $11 face mask. Another $8 coffee. $14 lunch she didn't pack. $19 plant she didn't need.

She scrolls back further. The charges keep coming. Small, scattered, easy to miss individually.

She opens her calculator and adds them up.

$620.

In one month.

Mia stares at the number. She's freelance—her income is inconsistent, and $620 is more than she made in her slowest week last month. That's rent money. That's a full month of groceries. That's her quarterly tax payment.

She looks at each charge again, trying to remember what triggered it.

The $8 coffee: stressful client call. The $22 book: finished a project, wanted to celebrate. The $15 subscription box: an ad that promised "self-care." The $18 candle: bad day. The $11 face mask: good day. The $19 plant: it was Tuesday.

She realizes: I wasn't buying things. I was buying permission to not think about money for ten minutes.

Every purchase was a "treat yourself" moment. But when you treat yourself every other day, it's not treating. It's just spending.

She thinks about the language she's been seeing everywhere—on Instagram, in ads, in influencer posts: You deserve this. Invest in yourself. Self-care isn't selfish. Life's too short.

None of it's wrong. She does deserve good things. But somewhere along the way, "treat yourself" stopped being about rewards and became a reflex. A reaction to stress, boredom, exhaustion, or just Tuesday.

Mia closes her banking app and opens Instagram. She unfollows eight accounts that post daily "treat yourself" content. Not because they're bad people. Because she can't afford to keep reacting to them.

Jordan's Deeper Realization

After her $340 weekend, Jordan starts paying attention to what she's seeing.

She's been following a few personal finance accounts on TikTok—people who post about paying off debt, saving money, building wealth. It feels motivating at first. Inspiring, even.

Then she notices something.

One account: "I paid off $80K in debt in two years!" Another: "I bought my first house at 25!" Another: "I'm 27 and have $200K saved!"

Jordan's impressed. She wants that. She starts comparing her own progress—her student loans, her $1,200 in savings, no house, no six-figure net worth. She's 23. She feels behind.

Then she clicks on one of the accounts. Scrolls back through their old posts. And finds the context they didn't mention in the viral video.

The person who paid off $80K in debt? They lived with their parents rent-free for two years and made $95K/year.

The person who bought a house at 25? Their parents covered the down payment.

The person with $200K saved at 27? They inherited $60K and had no student loans.

Jordan sits with this for a minute.

None of these things are bad. People should use whatever advantages they have. But the viral posts don't show the advantages. They just show the ending. The win. The number that makes you feel like you're failing by comparison.

Everyone shows their ending. Nobody shows their beginning.

She thinks about her own situation. She's paying her own rent. She has student loans. She doesn't have family money. Her timeline is going to be different than someone who started with a $60K inheritance. And that's okay.

She opens her settings and starts unfollowing accounts. Not all of them—just the ones that make her feel like she's losing a race she didn't know she was running. She follows new accounts instead. People documenting the middle of their journey, not just the end. People being honest about their advantages and their setbacks.

It feels different. Less like a highlight reel. More like real life.

Protecting Yourself (Without Deleting Everything)

You don't have to quit social media. You have to stop letting it run your finances.

Audit your feed. Unfollow or mute accounts that make you feel inadequate, promote unrealistic lifestyles without acknowledging their advantages, or consistently push you toward spending. You control what you consume. Emma unfollowed fifteen accounts in ten minutes and her feed felt different within a day.

Follow intentionally. If you're going to be on social media, make it work for you. Look for legitimate personal finance educators (check credentials, not follower counts), people documenting realistic journeys, and content that makes you think rather than want.

Add friction between scrolling and spending. The path from seeing something to buying it is designed to be frictionless. Add friction back.

The Friction Toolkit

Tactic	What It Does
Remove saved payment info from social shopping apps	Adds steps between impulse and purchase
Unlink social media from shopping (Instagram Shop, TikTok Shop)	Breaks the one-tap pipeline
Screenshot instead of clicking "buy"	Forces a 48-hour cooling period
Never buy directly through social media	Makes you research price and alternatives first
48-hour rule for anything over $50	Kills most impulse purchases

Mia implemented this system and went from 23 impulse purchases in a month to 2. That's a 91% reduction—not from willpower, but from friction.

Set boundaries. Time limits on apps (most phones have this built in). No scrolling in the first hour after waking or the last hour before bed. No scrolling when you're emotionally vulnerable—stressed, bored, lonely, or celebrating. Those are the moments the algorithm hits hardest.

Reality-check your "normal." Spend time with actual people in real life. When you're with friends in person, you see the full picture—the bills they stress about, the trade-offs they make, the things they can't afford. That context disappears on social media. Jordan called a friend and spent three hours just talking. No photos. No posts. She drove home and realized: this is the actual normal. Nobody posts this.

Find real community. Online communities around budgeting, debt payoff, and investing can provide genuine support—encouragement during hard stretches, practical advice from people in similar situations, accountability, and celebration of milestones that don't cost anything. The difference between these communities and influencer content is simple: nobody's selling you anything. Subreddits like r/personalfinance and r/financialindependence are decent starting points.

Social media isn't going away. The algorithms will keep getting smarter, the ads will keep getting more targeted, and the pressure to spend will keep showing up in your feed disguised as normal life.

The feed is not reality. The platforms profit from your insecurity. Comparison is rigged. You control your feed. You can add friction. You can use it intentionally.

Your financial journey doesn't need to look good on Instagram. It just needs to work for you.

Your Move

- **Today:** Unfollow five accounts that consistently make you feel inadequate or trigger spending.
- **This week:** Remove saved payment info from Instagram, TikTok, and any app where you've impulse-bought.
- **This month:** Track every purchase triggered by social media for 30 days. Add it up. That's your number. Jordan's was $7,200/year. What's yours?

When It Goes Sideways

"I keep spending money I don't have because of what I see online."

What happened: Jordan's $340 weekend wasn't a one-time thing. Over three months, she tracked $1,800 in spending she could directly trace to social media — clothes from Instagram ads, restaurants from friends' stories, products from TikTok, concert tickets from FOMO. That's $600/month, or $7,200/year — more than she pays in student loan payments annually. She wasn't shopping because she needed things. She was reacting to a feed designed to make her feel like she was missing out.

Why it happens: Social media collapses the distance between desire and action. You see something, you want it, you buy it — often in under 60 seconds. There's no drive to the store, no time to reconsider, no friction at all. Add in an algorithm that learns exactly what triggers your spending and serves you more of it, and you've got a system that's optimized to drain your bank account while making you feel like every purchase was your idea.

What to do: Jordan implements the full friction toolkit: removes saved payment info from all social shopping, unlinks Instagram and TikTok from shopping features, sets a 48-hour screenshot rule for anything she wants to buy, and deletes shopping apps from her phone entirely. She sets daily time limits on social media apps — 30 minutes each. She unfollows or mutes 40+ accounts that trigger spending. Then she tracks her social-media-driven spending for one month to see the actual impact. The goal isn't perfection — it's awareness and friction. Making it harder to buy on impulse cuts most of the damage.

What not to do: Delete all social media in a burst of guilt and then re-download everything a week later. Extreme reactions don't stick. Also, don't just "try to have more willpower" — willpower doesn't beat an algorithm backed by billions in engineering. Change your environment instead of relying on discipline. And don't feel guilty about past spending — guilt doesn't fix anything. Systems do.

"All my friends seem way ahead of me financially and I feel like a failure."

What happened: Michael follows a bunch of people from college on social media. Two of them just bought houses. One posts about her investment portfolio hitting $100K. Another travels constantly and always has new clothes. Michael has $8,000 in credit card debt, a car he's underwater on, and $2,100 in savings. He feels like he's the only one who's struggling. He's started avoiding social situations because he can't keep up.

Why it happens: Social media flattens context. Michael sees the house purchase but not the parents who gave $40,000 for the down payment. He sees the $100K portfolio but not the $85,000 tech salary and zero student loans that made it possible. He sees the travel posts but not the $22,000 in credit card debt behind them. Everyone broadcasts their wins. Almost nobody posts about their advantages, their debt, or their struggles. Michael is comparing his behind-the-scenes to everyone else's highlight reel.

What to do: Michael takes a break from the accounts that make him feel worst — not forever, just a reset. He writes down where he was six months ago versus where he is now: his credit card balance is down $1,400, his emergency fund exists where it didn't before, and he's contributing to his 401(k) for the first time. That's real progress, even though it wouldn't make a flashy social media post. He starts following accounts that document realistic financial journeys — people paying off debt, building from zero, making mistakes and recovering. And he talks to one real friend honestly about money. He'll almost certainly discover they're dealing with more than their feed suggests.

What not to do: Increase spending to keep up appearances. Michael already knows where that leads — it's how he got $8,000 in credit card debt in the first place. Also, don't isolate. Avoiding friends because you feel behind makes the comparison worse, not better. Real friendships survive honest conversations about money. And don't assume everyone who looks successful actually is — some of those "ahead" friends will be in this book's target audience within a few years when the bills come due.

"My teenager/younger sibling is already falling into the social media spending trap."

Emma's younger sister (19, college freshman) asked to borrow $300 for "essentials." The list: a Stanley cup, specific skincare products from TikTok, and a subscription box. She'd already burned through her work-study paycheck on similar purchases and was dipping into the textbook savings account their parents set up.

This one's tricky, because the instinct is to lecture. Don't.

Emma's sister doesn't see these as luxuries. In her social circle, they're baseline. When every person in your feed has the same water bottle, the same skincare, the same aesthetic, opting out feels like a social risk — not a financial decision. The spending isn't really about the products. It's about belonging. And telling a 19-year-old that belonging doesn't matter is a guaranteed way to get ignored.

What works better: make the invisible costs visible without making her feel stupid. Emma shows her sister the annual number — $300/month is $3,600/year, more than a semester of textbooks. She helps her build a simple budget with a "fun money" line — $75/month for whatever she wants, no judgment — so the spending has a boundary instead of a ban. She shares her own money mistakes at 19. And she asks one question: "A year from now, would you rather have all those products or $3,600 in savings?"

Don't lend the $300. Don't dismiss the social pressure as shallow. Don't try to ban social media. And don't expect one conversation to fix it — this is a long game of gradually shifting someone's relationship with spending and social validation. The fact that Emma is even having the conversation puts her sister further ahead than most.

Social media isn't going away. The algorithms will keep getting smarter, the ads will keep getting more targeted, and the pressure to spend will keep showing up in your feed disguised as normal life.

You can't win by fighting the algorithm with willpower. You win by changing the environment: more friction between you and impulse purchases, less time on the platforms that trigger spending, and an honest accounting of what your feed is actually costing you. Jordan's $7,200/year in social-media-driven spending wasn't a character flaw. It was a system working exactly as designed — just not in her favor.

Build a better system. The algorithm doesn't stand a chance against someone who's paying attention.

Conclusion: Your Financial Game Plan

> *"The best time to start was yesterday. The second best time is now." —Unknown*

Tyler checked his savings app on a Wednesday morning before his shift. He does this sometimes now—not obsessively, not anxiously, just a quick look the way you'd check the weather. The number said $680. Seven months ago, it said $0.

He locked his phone, put it in his locker, and clocked in. He didn't tell anyone. There was nothing to tell, really. He just had $680 that didn't exist before, a Roth IRA he'd never heard of a year ago, and a credit score that finally showed up when he searched for it.

Nothing about his life looked dramatically different from the outside. Same apartment with roommates. Different warehouse now—the distribution center across town, $16.80/hr after the forklift cert. Same truck. But something had shifted underneath all of it, quietly, the way compound interest works: slowly, then not so slowly.

He was eighteen and he had a foundation. Most people twice his age couldn't say that.

Here's where each of our five characters stands:

Tyler (18, warehouse → distribution center, $16.80/hr after his forklift certification) opened a Roth IRA with $50/month in a total market index fund. He has a secured credit card with a $300 limit that he uses for gas and pays off every month. His emergency fund hit $500 and kept going — it's at $680 now. He's building from zero, and he's building.

Jordan (23, marketing, $52K after her raise) set up a zero-based budget, enrolled in her company's 401(k) at 6% to get the full match, and switched her investments from three high-fee funds to a single S&P 500 index fund. She implemented the social media friction toolkit and cut her impulse spending by $450/month. She's putting that toward her $34,000 in student loans using the avalanche method. Her credit score is up to 705.

Mia (21, gig worker) opened a separate tax savings account and now transfers 30% of every payment the day it arrives. She set quarterly tax reminders and filed on time. She audited her subscriptions and cut $135/month in recurring charges. She's building an emergency fund sized for her variable income — targeting $7,200 (three months at her low-income baseline). She's at $2,100.

Michael (26, IT, $55K) stopped using credit cards entirely while paying down his $8,000 balance — now at $6,600 using the avalanche method. He said no to the dealer who wanted to roll his negative equity into a new loan. He set up a zero-based budget with a "car costs" line that accounts for the real $840/month his car costs. He started a $75/month car maintenance sinking fund. His credit score has climbed from 640 to 668 as his utilization drops.

Emma (24, federal GS-9, $68K) switched her TSP contributions from Traditional to Roth after running the tax math from Chapter 7, then bumped her contribution from 5% to 8%. She's in the L 2065 Fund. She completed a will, healthcare directive, and financial power of attorney for $165 and a Saturday afternoon. She's making income-driven payments on her student loans while building toward PSLF. Her emergency fund sits at $8,400 — five months of bare-bones expenses.

None of them are "done." All of them are further than they were.

You don't have to do everything at once. You don't have to be perfect. You just have to start — and keep going.

The Order of Operations

Personal finance feels overwhelming because everything seems urgent at once. Emergency fund! Pay off debt! Invest! Build credit! Save for a house!

Here's the order that makes the most sense for most people:

Level 1: Stop the Bleeding

Do this first, no matter what.

1. **Make a basic budget.** Know what's coming in and going out. You can't fix what you can't see. *(Chapter 3)*
2. **Pay minimums on everything.** Don't default. Don't let anything go to collections. Late payments trash your credit and trigger fees that make everything harder. *(Chapter 5)*
3. **Build a starter emergency fund ($500–$1,000).** High-yield savings account, separate from checking. This prevents small emergencies from becoming debt spirals. *(Chapter 4)*

Level 2: Build the Foundation

1. **Get your employer's full 401(k)/TSP match.** Free money — 100% instant return. If your employer matches up to 5%, contribute at least 5%. For most young people, choose the Roth option if available. *(Chapter 7)*
2. **Pay off high-interest debt.** Credit cards, payday loans, BNPL balances — anything above 8%. Attack aggressively using avalanche (highest interest first) or snowball (smallest balance first). *(Chapter 5)*
3. **Grow your emergency fund to 3 months of expenses.** Keep it at a different bank than your checking to reduce temptation. *(Chapter 4)*

Level 3: Accelerate

1. **Max out tax-advantaged accounts in this order:**

- 401(k)/TSP up to the full employer match (you did this in Level 2)
- Roth IRA up to $7,500 (2026) — more investment choices and flexibility
- HSA if you have one — triple tax advantage *(Chapter 7)*
- Back to 401(k)/TSP toward the $24,500 limit (2026)

2. **Pay off moderate-interest debt (5–8%).** Student loans, car loans. Some people prefer to invest instead if rates are low — either approach is reasonable. Run the math. *(Chapter 5)*
3. **Build emergency fund to 6 months.** Especially important for self-employed, variable income, or unstable industries. *(Chapter 4)*

Level 4: Build Wealth

1. **Invest in a taxable brokerage account.** Once tax-advantaged accounts are maxed, keep investing in low-cost index funds. Set up automatic contributions. *(Chapter 7)*
2. **Save for big goals.** House down payment, business, early retirement — whatever your version of winning looks like. Sinking funds for goals under 5 years; invest for longer-term goals. *(Chapter 9)*
3. **Give generously.** If that's important to you, you're now in a position to do it meaningfully.

The Simple System

Automate Everything

The best financial system doesn't require willpower. Set it up once, let it run.

Direct deposit splits — send a percentage to savings before you ever see it. **Automatic 401(k)/TSP contributions** — start with the match, increase 1% every year or every raise. **Automatic Roth IRA contributions** — even $150/week gets close to the annual max. **Automatic transfers** to savings, HSA, and sinking funds right after payday. **Autopay for bills** — never miss a payment, never pay a late fee.

When saving and investing happen automatically, you don't have to decide to do it every month. The decision is made once.

The Monthly Money Date

Once a month, 30–60 minutes. Put it on your calendar.

Review last month's spending for surprises. Check progress toward goals. Adjust budget categories if needed. Review upcoming irregular expenses. Make sure automated systems are running. Celebrate wins — even small ones.

This isn't about obsessing over every dollar. It's about staying aware and catching problems early.

The Annual Checkup

Once a year, do a deeper review (Chapter 10): update beneficiaries, review insurance, check credit reports, reassess goals, adjust your plan as life changes. Pick a consistent time — birthday, New Year's, tax season — and make it a habit.

Milestones (Rough Guide, Not Rules)

By 18–25 (Early Career): Emergency fund started. Contributing enough for the employer match. No high-interest debt (or actively paying it down). Basic budget in place. Credit score established.

By 26–30 (Establishing): Emergency fund at 3–6 months. Retirement savings roughly 1x salary by 30 (aggressive but a good target). High-interest debt eliminated. Credit score 670+.

By 30–35 (Building): Retirement savings 1–2x salary. Maxing or close to maxing tax-advantaged accounts. Net worth growing consistently. Insurance and legal documents in place.

Reality check: The median net worth for Americans under 35 is around $39,000. If you have a positive net worth and are saving consistently, you're doing better than many. And the only comparison that matters is whether you're better off than last year.

When You Mess Up

You will. Everyone does.

Don't catastrophize. One bad month doesn't erase progress. One impulse purchase doesn't mean you're bad with money.

Get back on track immediately. The worst thing after a slip-up is giving up for the rest of the month. That turns a $200 mistake into a $2,000 mistake. Messed up Tuesday? Get back on track Wednesday.

Look for patterns. If you keep slipping the same way, that's data — maybe your budget is unrealistic, maybe you have a trigger you haven't addressed, maybe you need more friction.

Forgive yourself. Financial shame is counterproductive. You're learning. That puts you ahead of most people.

What's Next

You have the knowledge now. You know more about personal finance than most adults — including many who are older and earn more.

But knowledge without action is just trivia.

Today: Pick one thing from this book and do it. Check your credit score. Set up a savings transfer. Look at your 401(k) options. Review your subscriptions. Something.

This week: Make a basic budget if you don't have one.

This month: Identify which level of the Order of Operations you're on. What's your next step?

This year: Build momentum. Small actions compound — just like interest.

You're not behind. You're not broken. You're not bad with money — you just hadn't learned this stuff yet.

Now you have.

Spend less than you earn. Save the difference. Invest for the future. Protect what you build.

Do that consistently, for years, and you'll be fine. Better than fine.

You've got this.

Bonus Resources

Quick Reference Guides

The Financial Order of Operations (Cheat Sheet)

Not sure where your next dollar should go? Follow this order:

1. **401(k)/TSP up to employer/agency match** – Free money. Never skip this.
2. **Build a $1,000 starter emergency fund** – Your first buffer against life.
3. **Pay off high-interest debt (8%+)** – Credit cards, payday loans, high-rate personal loans.
4. **Grow emergency fund to 3 months of expenses** – Real security starts here.
5. **Max out Roth IRA ($7,500 in 2026)** – Tax-free growth for decades.
6. **Max out HSA if available ($4,400 individual / $8,750 family in 2026)** – Triple tax advantage.
7. **Increase 401(k)/TSP to max ($24,500 in 2026)** – Reduce taxes, build wealth.
8. **Build emergency fund to 6 months** – Full protection before tackling moderate debt.
9. **Pay off moderate-interest debt (4-7%)** – Car loans, some student loans.
10. **Taxable brokerage investing** – Build wealth beyond tax-advantaged limits.
11. **Extra mortgage payments** – Optional, depending on rate and goals.

Key Numbers to Know (2026)

Retirement Contribution Limits:

Account	Limit	Catch-Up
401(k) / TSP	$24,500	$32,500 if 50+; $35,750 if 60-63
IRA (Traditional or Roth)	$7,500	$8,600 if 50+
HSA (Individual)	$4,400	+$1,000 if 55+
HSA (Family)	$8,750	+$1,000 if 55+

Roth IRA Income Limits (2026):

Filing Status	Full Contribution	Phase-Out Range
Single	Up to $153,000	$153,000-$168,000
Married filing jointly	Up to $242,000	$242,000-$252,000

Federal Tax Brackets (2026, Single Filers):

Rate	Income Range
10%	$0-$12,400
12%	$12,401-$50,400
22%	$50,401-$105,700
24%	$105,701-$201,775
32%	$201,776-$256,225
35%	$256,226-$640,600
37%	$640,601+

Standard Deduction (2026):

Filing Status	Deduction
Single	$16,100
Married filing jointly	$32,200
Head of household	$24,150

Social Security and Medicare Tax (2026): Social Security is 6.2% (up to $184,500 wage base). Medicare is 1.45% (no limit). Self-employed pay both halves (15.3% total).

Budget Percentages (Guidelines, Not Rules)

The 50/30/20 Framework: 50% needs (housing, utilities, groceries, insurance, minimum debt payments), 30% wants (entertainment, dining, hobbies, subscriptions), 20% savings and extra debt payments.

Housing: Aim for 25-30% of take-home pay (rent + utilities). Mortgage: keep total housing costs under 28% of gross income.

Transportation: Total car costs (payment + insurance + gas + maintenance) should stay under 15-20% of take-home.

Emergency Fund Targets: Starter: $1,000. Stable job, low expenses: 3 months of expenses. Variable income, high expenses, or dependents: 6+ months.

Resources for Specific Communities

For First-Generation Wealth Builders

- **First-Gen Investing** (firstgeninvesting.com) — Community and education for those without family financial guidance. If you're the first person in your family to open a brokerage account or negotiate a salary, this is built for you. The content assumes nothing and judges nothing.
- **r/personalfinance and r/povertyfinance** — Reddit communities with supportive advice for all income levels. r/personalfinance skews toward people with stable incomes optimizing their money. r/povertyfinance is better if you're working with very little and need advice that respects that reality. Both are free, anonymous, and surprisingly helpful.

For Women

- **Ellevest** — Investment platform designed with women's financial realities in mind. The fee is slightly higher than Vanguard or Fidelity, but the planning tools account for wage gaps, career breaks, and longer lifespans. If you want an investing platform that doesn't pretend the gender pay gap doesn't exist, this is it.

- **Her First $100K** — Financial education focused on women's wealth building. Tori Dunlap built this brand around the idea that women shouldn't feel weird about wanting money. Good content on negotiation, investing basics, and fighting the "women are bad with money" narrative.

For BIPOC Communities

- **The Budgetnista** (thebudgetnista.com) — Tiffany Aliche's platform focused on financial education. She's one of the best in the game at making money concepts feel accessible without dumbing them down. Her "Live Richer Challenge" is a good starting point if you want structured steps.
- **Melanin Money** — Financial podcast and community. Covers investing, entrepreneurship, and wealth building with cultural context that mainstream finance media tends to skip.
- **National Endowment for Financial Education** — Free resources in multiple languages. Useful if English isn't your first language or if you're helping family members who need materials in Spanish, Mandarin, or other languages.

For LGBTQ+ Individuals

- **Pride Financial** — Resources addressing unique financial planning needs. Tax implications of marriage, adoption costs, estate planning for non-traditional families — the stuff that generic financial advice doesn't cover.
- **Equality Federation** — List of LGBTQ+-affirming financial planners. If you're going to pay someone for financial advice, you want someone who understands your life without needing a tutorial.

For Immigrants and International Workers

- **Immigrantfinance.com** — Navigating U.S. financial systems as an immigrant. Covers everything from building credit without a credit history to understanding tax obligations when you have ties to more than one country. If the U.S. financial system feels like it was designed for people who aren't you, this helps translate.

- **ITIN information** (IRS.gov) — For those without Social Security numbers. You can still file taxes, build a financial record, and in some cases open bank accounts with an ITIN. The IRS cares about collecting taxes from everyone — which means the system has a path for you even if it doesn't advertise it.

For People with Disabilities

- **ABLE accounts** — Tax-advantaged savings that don't affect benefits eligibility. If you receive SSI or SSDI, most savings accounts can threaten your benefits. ABLE accounts let you save up to $100,000 without that penalty. Hugely underused.
- **Disability Rights Legal Center** — Financial planning resources tailored to the intersection of disability benefits and wealth building. Navigating SSI asset limits, SSDI work incentives, and special needs trusts requires specialized knowledge.

Low-Income and Crisis Resources

- **211.org** — Local resources for food, housing, and financial assistance. Dial 2-1-1 from any phone or visit the website. They connect you with resources in your area that you probably don't know exist — utility assistance, food banks, rent help, free legal aid.
- **Benefits.gov** — Check eligibility for government assistance programs. Answer a few questions and it tells you what you qualify for. A lot of people leave money on the table because they don't realize they're eligible.
- **VITA (Volunteer Income Tax Assistance)** — Free tax preparation for people making under $67,000. IRS-certified volunteers do your taxes for free. No catch. If you're paying

TurboTax $80 and your return is straightforward, this is a better option. ## Recommended Tools and Resources

Budgeting Apps

App	Best For	Cost
YNAB (You Need A Budget)	Intentional zero-based budgeting	$99/year (free for students)
Credit Karma	Automatic tracking, free credit scores	Free
Goodbudget	Digital envelope system, couples	Free (limited) / $80/year
EveryDollar	Simple zero-based budgeting	Free (limited) / $79.99/year
Copilot	Beautiful interface, iOS users	$70/year

A few notes: YNAB has a learning curve, but the people who stick with it tend to become evangelists — it fundamentally changes how you think about money. The $99/year price tag pays for itself fast if you're the type who needs structure. Credit Karma is free because they make money recommending financial products to you, so take their "suggestions" with a grain of salt — but the tracking and free credit scores are legitimately useful. If you and a partner are budgeting together, Goodbudget's shared envelope system is worth trying before you pay for anything.

Apps change frequently. Research current options before committing.

Investment Platforms

Best for Beginners: Fidelity (no minimums, excellent service, zero-fee index funds), Charles Schwab (no minimums, great research tools, physical branches), Vanguard (the original low-cost indexing pioneer, best for buy-and-hold).

Honest take: any of these three will serve you well for decades. The differences between them are minor. Fidelity has the best app and the lowest-cost funds. Schwab is great if you want to walk into a branch and talk to a human. Vanguard's interface is clunky but their investment philosophy is why index fund investing exists at all. Pick one, open an account, and stop researching. The best platform is the one you actually use.

Robo-Advisors (Hands-Off Investing): Betterment (automatic investing and rebalancing, 0.25% annual fee), Wealthfront (similar, includes financial planning tools), Fidelity Go / Schwab Intelligent Portfolios (robo options from traditional brokerages).

Robo-advisors are worth it if the alternative is not investing at all. If you know you won't log in and rebalance your portfolio yourself, paying 0.25% for someone (or something) to do it automatically is a reasonable trade. But if you're comfortable buying a single target-date fund or total market index fund, you don't need a robo-advisor — you'd be paying a fee for automation you can set up yourself in 15 minutes.

Index Funds Worth Knowing About

These are examples, not recommendations. Expense ratios are subject to change. Verify current rates before investing.

S&P 500:

Provider	Fund	Expense Ratio
Fidelity	FXAIX	0.015%
Vanguard	VOO / VFIAX	0.03% / 0.04%
Schwab	SWPPX	0.02%

Total U.S. Stock Market:

Provider	Fund	Expense Ratio
Fidelity	FSKAX / FZROX	0.015% / 0%
Vanguard	VTI / VTSAX	0.03% / 0.04%
Schwab	SWTSX	0.03%

Total International:

Provider	Fund	Expense Ratio
Fidelity	FTIHX	0.06%
Vanguard	VXUS / VTIAX	0.08% / 0.12%
Schwab	SWISX	0.06%

Total Bond Market:

Provider	Fund	Expense Ratio
Fidelity	FXNAX	0.025%
Vanguard	BND / VBTLX	0.03% / 0.05%
Schwab	SCHZ	0.03%

TSP Funds (Federal Employees and Military):

Fund	What It Tracks	Expense Ratio
C Fund	S&P 500	0.049%
S Fund	U.S. Small/Mid Cap	0.049%
I Fund	International	0.049%
F Fund	U.S. Bonds	0.049%
G Fund	Government Securities	0.049%
L Funds	Lifecycle (Target Date)	0.049%

High-Yield Savings Accounts

Rates change frequently based on Federal Reserve decisions. As of writing, competitive HYSAs offer 4-5% APY. Compare current rates at Bankrate.com or NerdWallet.

Consistently competitive options: Marcus by Goldman Sachs, Ally Bank, Capital One 360, Discover Savings, American Express Savings, Wealthfront Cash Account, SoFi.

The most important thing isn't which HYSA you pick — it's that your emergency fund isn't sitting in a regular savings account earning 0.01%. The difference between 0.01% and 4.5% on a $5,000 emergency fund is roughly $225/year. That's free money for a 10-minute account setup. Ally and Marcus tend to have the most consistently competitive rates without gimmicky teaser promotions that drop after six months.

Credit Monitoring and Reports

Free Credit Reports: AnnualCreditReport.com is the official source, with free weekly reports from all three bureaus.

Free Credit Scores: Credit Karma (free VantageScore from TransUnion and Equifax). Most bank and credit card apps now show free FICO or VantageScore.

Credit Freeze Links:

- Equifax (equifax.com/personal/credit-report-services/)
- Experian (experian.com/freeze)
- TransUnion (transunion.com/credit-freeze).

Tax Filing

Free Options: IRS Free File (income limits apply, irs.gov/freefile), IRS Direct File (limited states, directfile.irs.gov), Cash App Taxes (free federal and state). *Subject to government changes.*

Paid Options: TurboTax, H&R Block, TaxAct ($0-$200+ depending on complexity). CPA or tax professional ($150-$500+, worth it for complex situations).

Financial Calculators

- **Compound Interest:** investor.gov/financial-tools-calculators/calculators/compound-interest-calculator
- **Rent vs. Buy:** nytimes.com/interactive/2014/upshot/buy-rent-calculator.html
- **401(k) Calculator:** bankrate.com/retirement/calculators/401-k-retirement-calculator/

- **Debt Payoff:** undebt.it (free debt snowball/avalanche calculator)
- **Tax Withholding:** irs.gov/individuals/tax-withholding-estimator ## Essential Documents Checklist

Documents to Create

Document	Purpose	Done?
Will	Who gets your stuff, who handles your estate	☐
Healthcare Directive	Your medical wishes if incapacitated	☐
Healthcare Power of Attorney	Who makes medical decisions for you	☐
HIPAA Authorization	Who can access your medical records	☐
Financial Power of Attorney	Who handles your finances if you cannot	☐

Information to Organize

Item	Done?
List of all accounts with account numbers	☐
List of all debts with account numbers	☐
Insurance policies with policy numbers	☐
Beneficiary designations for all accounts	☐
Login credentials stored securely	☐
Location of important physical documents	☐

Beneficiary Review

Account Type	Primary Beneficiary	Contingent Beneficiary	Last Updated
401(k) / TSP	____________	____________	________
IRA	____________	____________	________

Account Type	Primary Beneficiary	Contingent Beneficiary	Last Updated
Roth IRA	______________	______________	__________
Life Insurance	______________	______________	__________
HSA	______________	______________	__________
Bank Accounts (POD)	______________	______________	__________
Brokerage (TOD)	______________	______________	__________

Sample Scripts and Letters

Scripts and Templates

The negotiation scripts and letter templates are now located in the chapters where you'll need them:

- **Credit card rate negotiation** — Chapter 5 (Debt)
- **Credit limit increase request** — Chapter 6 (Credit Scores)
- **Credit report dispute letter** — Chapter 6 (Credit Scores)
- **Debt validation letter** — Chapter 5 (Debt)

Review and Update

Task	Done?
Check all beneficiary designations	☐
Review insurance coverage	☐
Pull credit reports from all three bureaus	☐
Check credit score for issues	☐
Review subscriptions and recurring charges	☐
Update budget categories if needed	☐

Assess Progress

Task	Done?
Calculate net worth (assets minus debts)	☐
Review retirement account balances	☐
Check emergency fund level	☐
Review debt balances	☐
Assess progress toward goals	☐

Plan Ahead and Protect

Task	Done?
Set or review goals for the coming year	☐
Adjust retirement contributions if income changed	☐
Plan for major expenses (create sinking funds)	☐
Review tax withholding	☐
Update passwords for financial accounts	☐
Verify credit freezes are in place	☐
Review essential documents for updates	☐

Glossary of Terms

Amortization: Spreading loan payments over time, where early payments are mostly interest and later payments are mostly principal.

APR (Annual Percentage Rate): The yearly interest rate on borrowed money, including fees.

APY (Annual Percentage Yield): The yearly return on savings, including compound interest.

Asset: Something you own that has value (cash, investments, property, car).

Bear Market: Falling prices, typically defined as a 20%+ decline from recent highs.

Beneficiary: The person designated to receive your account or insurance proceeds when you die.

Brokerage Account: An account for buying and selling investments.

Bull Market: Rising prices, indicating investor optimism and economic strength.

Capital Gains: Profit from selling an investment for more than you paid. Short-term (held under 1 year) taxed as income; long-term (held over 1 year) taxed at lower rates.

Compound Interest: Interest on both principal and accumulated interest. The snowball effect that makes early investing powerful.

Cost Basis: The original value of an asset for tax purposes, usually the purchase price.

Credit Report: A detailed history of your credit accounts, payment history, and inquiries. You have three (one from each bureau).

Credit Score: A number (300-850) predicting how likely you are to repay debt.

Credit Utilization: The percentage of available credit you are using. Aim for under 30%, ideally under 10%.

Deductible: The amount you pay out of pocket before insurance kicks in.

Diversification: Spreading investments across different assets to reduce risk.

Dividend: A payment from a company to shareholders, usually from profits.

Dollar-Cost Averaging (DCA): Investing a fixed amount at regular intervals regardless of market conditions.

Emergency Fund: Cash savings for unexpected expenses or income loss. Typically 3-6 months of expenses.

Equity: The value of ownership. Home equity = home value minus mortgage balance.

Expense Ratio: The annual fee charged by a mutual fund or ETF, as a percentage. Lower is better.

FDIC: Federal Deposit Insurance Corporation. Insures bank deposits up to $250,000 per depositor, per bank.

FICO Score: The most widely used credit score (300-850).

Fiduciary: A person legally required to act in your best interest. Fee-only financial advisors are fiduciaries; commission-based salespeople typically are not.

Gross Income: Your total earnings before taxes and deductions.

HSA (Health Savings Account): Tax-advantaged account for medical expenses with high-deductible health plans. Triple tax benefit.

Index Fund: A fund that tracks a market index rather than trying to beat it.

Inflation Rate: The rate at which prices increase over time. The Fed targets approximately 2% annually.

IRA (Individual Retirement Account): Tax-advantaged retirement account you open yourself. Traditional = tax-deductible now, taxed later. Roth = taxed now, tax-free later.

Liability: Something you owe (debt, loans, credit card balances).

Liquidity: How quickly an asset converts to cash.

Marginal Tax Rate: The tax rate on your last dollar of income.

Effective Tax Rate: The actual percentage of total income that goes to taxes.

Net Income: Earnings after taxes and deductions. Also called take-home pay.

Net Worth: Total assets minus total liabilities. The single best measure of financial health.

POD (Payable on Death): Beneficiary designation for bank accounts that transfers funds directly upon death, avoiding probate.

Premium: The amount you pay for insurance coverage, usually monthly.

Principal: The original amount borrowed or invested, not including interest or returns.

Probate: The legal process of distributing a deceased person's assets. Can be slow and expensive.

Rebalancing: Adjusting your portfolio back to your target allocation.

Roth: A retirement account type (Roth IRA, Roth 401(k), Roth TSP) where contributions are taxed now but growth and withdrawals are tax-free.

SIPC: Securities Investor Protection Corporation. Protects brokerage holdings up to $500,000 if a brokerage fails.

Sinking Fund: Money set aside for a specific future expense.

Tax-Loss Harvesting: Selling investments at a loss to offset capital gains and reduce taxes.

TOD (Transfer on Death): Beneficiary designation for brokerage accounts that avoids probate.

Traditional: A retirement account type where contributions are tax-deductible now but taxed in retirement.

TSP (Thrift Savings Plan): The federal government's retirement savings plan for federal employees and military. Equivalent to a 401(k), with C, S, I, F, G, and L Funds.

Underwater: Owing more on a loan than the asset is worth.

Vesting: Earning ownership of employer-contributed retirement funds over time.

W-2: Tax form showing annual earnings and taxes withheld.

W-4: Form determining paycheck tax withholding.

Yield: The income return on an investment, as a percentage.

1099: Tax form reporting income other than wages. ## Books for Further Reading

What Comes Next

- *Intelligent Wealth* series by Joseph Maxim — If you've finished this book and you're ready for the next level — backdoor Roths, tax-loss harvesting, real estate analysis, FIRE math, business credit — this is where it picks up. Written for readers who've built the foundation and want to optimize. Same honest voice, higher stakes.

Personal Finance Foundations

- *I Will Teach You to Be Rich* by Ramit Sethi
- *The Simple Path to Wealth* by JL Collins
- *Your Money or Your Life* by Vicki Robin
- *The Psychology of Money* by Morgan Housel

Investing

- *The Little Book of Common Sense Investing* by John C. Bogle
- *A Random Walk Down Wall Street* by Burton Malkiel
- *The Bogleheads Guide to Investing*

Debt and Recovery

- *The Total Money Makeover* by Dave Ramsey (take investing advice with a grain of salt)
- *Broke Millennial* by Erin Lowry

Building Wealth

- *The Millionaire Next Door* by Thomas J. Stanley
- *Die With Zero* by Bill Perkins

Financial Independence

- *Playing with FIRE* by Scott Rieckens
- *Quit Like a Millionaire* by Kristy Shen

Preview: Intelligent Wealth

You've built the foundation. Emergency fund in place, debt under control, retirement contributions flowing, credit moving in the right direction. That puts you ahead of most people – but it's not the finish line.

At some point, the basics stop being enough. You max out your Roth IRA and start wondering what else you can do with the money. You hear someone mention a "backdoor Roth" and realize there's a whole layer of tax strategy you haven't touched. You start thinking about real estate, or early retirement, or whether your side hustle could actually become something bigger. The questions get more complex, and the generic advice stops fitting.

That's where the **Intelligent Wealth** series picks up.

Intelligent Wealth is written for readers who've done the work in this book – or arrived at the same place on their own – and are ready for what comes next. Age matters less than readiness. If you've got the fundamentals handled and you're hungry to optimize, you're the target audience.

What's Inside

Advanced tax optimization is where most people leave serious money on the table. Backdoor Roth conversions, mega backdoor strategies, tax-loss harvesting, and figuring out which investments belong in which accounts – these aren't tricks for the ultra-wealthy. They're tools available to anyone earning above the Roth IRA income limits or anyone who's maxed out their basic retirement accounts and wants to keep going. We'll walk through each strategy with the same real-numbers approach you've seen in this book, so you can decide which ones actually apply to your situation.

Real estate as a wealth-building tool gets the honest treatment. Not the "passive income" fantasy from social media, and not the doom-and-gloom "renting is throwing money away" pressure from your parents' generation. We'll cover house hacking, rental property analysis with real math (including the costs nobody mentions in YouTube thumbnails), REITs versus physical property, and 1031 exchanges. You'll learn how to evaluate whether real estate belongs in your wealth-building plan — or whether you're better off putting that energy into index funds.

The path to financial independence goes beyond the standard "save 25x your expenses" formula. We'll dig into sequence-of-returns risk (the thing that can wreck your retirement in year one), healthcare costs before Medicare eligibility, building income streams that actually work, and how to design a life where work becomes optional rather than mandatory. The goal isn't just early retirement — it's having enough options that you're working because you want to, not because you have to.

Advanced strategies covers territory that most personal finance books either skip or oversimplify: credit optimization and maximizing rewards strategically, building business credit, alternative investments, the real math on whole life insurance (spoiler: it's more nuanced than "always buy term"), estate planning beyond basic wills, and negotiating the purchases and salaries that move the needle most.

Entrepreneurship and self-employment tackles starting a business while you're still employed, self-employment tax optimization (Mia, this one's for you), retirement accounts designed for business owners — SEP IRAs, Solo 401(k)s, even defined benefit plans — and the real logistics of scaling a side hustle into a full-time operation.

Who It's For

If you've implemented the lessons in this book, you're ready. You don't need a six-figure salary or a finance degree. You need the habits, the foundation, and the willingness to learn strategies that are more complex but also more powerful.

Everything in Main Character Money was about getting your footing. Intelligent Wealth is about building from there — deliberately, strategically, and on your own terms.

Stay tuned.

www.ingramcontent.com/pod-product-compliance
Lightning Source LLC
LaVergne TN
LVHW022206200926
848481LV00006B/1866